CRYSTALS & L♥VE

CRYSTALS
& LOVE

Find your soul mate and unlock the power of love

JUDY HALL

GODSFIELD

An Hachette UK Company
www.hachette.co.uk

First published in Great Britain in 2007 by
Godsfield, an imprint of
Octopus Publishing Group Ltd,
Carmelite House,
50 Victoria Embankment,
London EC4Y 0DZ
www.octopusbooks.co.uk

This edition published in 2024.

Distributed in the US by
Hachette Book Group
1290 Avenue of the Americas
4th and 5th Floors
New York, NY 10104

Distributed in Canada by
Canadian Manda Group
664 Annette St.
Toronto, Ontario, Canada M6S 2C8

ISBN 978-1-8418-1582-4

A CIP catalogue record for this book is
available from the British Library.

Printed and bound in China

1 2 3 4 5 6 7 8 9 10

Publisher: Lucy Pessell
Designer: Isobel Platt
Editor: Feyi Oyesanya
Assistant Editor: Samina Rahman
Production Controller: Sumayyah Waheed

Disclaimer
All reasonable care has been taken in the
preparation of this book but the information
it contains is not intended to take the
place of treatment by a qualified medical
practitioner. Before making any changes in
your health regime, always consult a doctor.
While all the therapies detailed in this book
are completely safe if done correctly, you
must seek professional advice if you are in
any doubt about any medical condition. Any
application of the ideas and information
contained in this book is at the reader's sole
discretion and risk.

CONTENTS

DISCOVERING LOVE CRYSTALS

love makes the world go round,
and crystals are love made visible

CRYSTAL LOVE

Whether you are looking for new romance or a fun night out, want to create the right energies for a passionate evening with your dream lover, or need to heal an old hurt that is blocking finding a new love, this book shows you how to harness crystal energies to open your heart to love and attract more love into your life.

Rose Quartz Heart

The clearer and happier you feel inside, the more joyous and loving your outer world becomes because love attracts love. As you read through this book you will find rituals and layouts to help you draw love into your life and to transform distressing feelings into positive emotions. You will also find affirmations to support love. Affirmations are an extremely potent way of attracting more love into your life. These are best done holding an appropriate crystal while you look into the reflection of your eyes in a mirror.

USING CRYSTALS

Large chunks or big clusters of crystal look extremely decorative while also acting as a magnet for love. But small crystals attract love, too, and many of the crystals in this book look stunning when worn. This is an excellent way to draw crystal energy into your life – a Rose Quartz choker, for instance, adds a seductive element to a first date or romantic dinner. You can also keep a crystal in your pocket, or place it on your body and relax for 15 minutes for a fast recharge of love energy. Crystals tucked under your pillow at night work while you sleep – simply hold them for a few moments and ask them to help you throughout the night.

Amethyst Violet Flower

Crystals radiate energy continuously, but remember that they absorb energy too, and need regular cleansing (see page 14). When using stones for layouts, if the crystal has a point place it pointing away from the body to draw off negative energy or pointing inwards to draw in beneficial energy.

TIMING OF RITUALS

Traditionally the power of the moon was used to enhance rituals. Rituals to attract something new into your life are best done on a new moon. Rituals to let something go out of your life are best carried out at full moon.

FINDING YOUR LOVE CRYSTALS

You will discover that crystals are eager to help you find love. They jump into your hands in shops, friends suddenly gift you one, or you pick up a beautiful stone on a beach that becomes your love ally – not all 'crystals' are sparkly gemstones, most look more like lumps of rock.

Pick a crystal from the photographs throughout this book or, if you prefer, dowse for it (see page 12). You can also choose from the crystals listed under the various topics, or consult the index. One particular crystal may combine different properties – if you look under several headings and the same crystal comes up, this is the one for you.

STONES OR GEMS?

Love crystals do not have to be expensive: pieces of raw or tumbled stone (smooth and round and usually opaque) are just as powerful as faceted gems. Remember that crystals come in all shapes and sizes, and biggest is not always best, nor is the most beautiful the most powerful. Polished or tumbled stones are often more comfortable to use than pointed ones, although faceted gems are ideal for jewellery.

Wear them, place them over your heart, position them in your environment or under your pillow, or take them as a gem essence (see page 16). Whatever you do, your crystals will surround you with love.

Raw Diamonds

DOWSING

Dowsing often brings the hidden benefits of a crystal to light. For example you may not be aware of what is preventing you from attracting the love of your life, but dowsing will work it out and a crystal will transform whatever is getting in the way.

THE DOWSING TECHNIQUE

All you need is a pendulum (a crystal one is ideal) and a steady hand.

1. Hold the pendulum between your thumb and forefinger, with about a hand's breadth of chain below. Tuck any spare chain into the palm of your hand or wrap it around your remaining fingers.

2. Swing the pendulum in a wide circle. As you do so, tell yourself:
   'This is "Yes".'

3. Then swing it backwards and forwards and tell yourself:
   'This is "No".'

4. Test it out by holding the pendulum over your other hand. Keeping the hand holding the pendulum perfectly still, say out loud:
   'My name is...' [giving the name you are known by].
   The pendulum will swing around in a circle to indicate 'yes'.

5. Then say out loud:
   'My name is...' [giving a false name].
   The pendulum will swing backwards and forwards to indicate 'no'.

DOWSING FOR YOUR LOVE CRYSTAL

To find a love crystal, simply hold the pendulum over the crystal and ask:
'Is this the right crystal for ... [fill in the blank with whatever you are asking the crystal to assist you with] at this time?'

If the swing of the pendulum is slow to start and very small, ask: 'Is there a better crystal for the purpose?' Dowsing will give you a 'yes' or 'no' answer to many other questions, too – including: 'Is this really the man/woman for me?'

CLEANSING AND PROGRAMMING CRYSTALS

People often wonder why a crystal they have bought from a shop doesn't have an instant effect. This is usually because they have forgotten two very important aspects of crystal attraction: cleansing and programming. Your crystal can only work when you have told it what you need.

CLEANSING YOUR CRYSTAL

Crystals absorb energies from the environment or from people handling them. This is why, when you first acquire your crystal, you need to cleanse it. You also need to cleanse it after using it.

Cleansing is simple. If the crystal is not delicate, layered, a cluster or friable (that is to say, it will not dissolve in water or be damaged by it), place it under running water for a few minutes and then stand it in the sun for several hours to re-energize. If it is delicate (see Directory, pages 108–125), place it overnight in grains of uncooked brown rice and stand it in the sun next day. You can also stand your crystal on a Quartz cluster or large Carnelian to cleanse and recharge it overnight but those stones will then need cleansing.

PROGRAMMING YOUR CRYSTAL

Crystals work best when they have been programmed for a specific desire because it harnesses your intent. When you have cleansed your crystal, spend a few moments dedicating it to your purpose. Be specific. If it is to attract love, for instance, hold it in your hands, focus on it and state out loud: 'This crystal is dedicated to bringing more love into my life.' If what you want is great sex, say so. If it is to draw off a distressing feeling, affirm: 'This crystal transforms my attitude to...'

If at any time you want to change the programme, cleanse the crystal and leave it in the sun before rededicating it.

GEM ESSENCES

Soft, gentle and safe, a gem essence carries the subtle vibration of the crystal and transfers it to your body. Rub a few drops of the essence on your wrists or over your heart or chakras (see pages 82–85) two or three times a day, or add a few drops to your bath water. You can also add a few drops to a spray bottle of water and spritz it around you – an excellent way to prepare you or your bedroom for a blissful sexual encounter.

MAKING A GEM ESSENCE

1. Cleanse the crystal, or crystals, thoroughly. Place in a clean glass bowl and cover with spring water. If the crystal is delicate, friable (meaning it crumbles or dissolves in water) or toxic, however, place the crystal in an inner glass bowl and pour the spring water into the outer bowl.

2. Stand the bowl in the sun for several hours, then bottle the essence with one-third brandy or vodka to preserve it. This way, it will keep for months, even years, providing it's kept in a cool, dark place. Remember to label the bottle.

ATTRACTING LOVE

crystals can bring more
love into your life

BRINGING LOVE INTO YOUR LIFE

Crystals are just waiting to bring more love into your life and nothing attracts love more effectively than Rose Quartz. Place a big chunk of this beautiful stone, programmed (see page 15) to bring an abundance of love into your life in the relationship corner of your home (see grid, page 9) or place it by your bed, and you won't have to wait long for love.

Rose Quartz is also a vital part of the 'Attracting love ritual' (see page 24) and the 'Attracting love affirmation'. Holding a piece of Rose Quartz, repeat the affirmation several times a day. (It is important that you phrase it in the present to bring it into manifestation.)

Attracting love affirmation: 'I attract love into my life, my life is full of love right now, my life is full of abundant love. I am a magnet for love.'

Love attracting crystals: Rose Quartz and Strawberry Quartz, Danburite, Rhodochrosite, Almandine Garnet, Kunzite, Larimar, Sugilite, Pink Tourmaline, Topaz, Ruby, Garnet, Green Aventurine (for love in later life).

SOUL MATE OR TWIN FLAME?

The soul mate crystal and the twin flame crystal look the same – they both comprise two crystals growing together from a common base – but have different effects according to the programming. Be very specific about which kind of love you want when programming your crystal.

A soul mate crystal will attract a soul mate into your life. Although most people think a soul mate is the perfect lover, your soul mate may actually help you learn some difficult lessons and your partnership may, therefore, appear to be a 'bad' relationship. It is only later that you appreciate what the gift was in learning that particular lesson. Fortunately even this kind of soul mate relationship benefits from the power of crystals but you may prefer to programme your crystal to attract a different kind of love.

A twin flame is an ideal relationship – like having a soul mate but without the drawbacks. A twin flame is a life companion who loves you unconditionally and offers mental empathy, emotional rapport, spiritual connection, unconditional support, friendship and blissful physical fulfilment. A twin flame crystal attracts someone who is totally compatible.

Soul Mate or Twin Flame Crystal

LOVE RITUALS

Rituals to attract love are highly potent. Many use romantic Rose Quartz, which has a surprisingly powerful effect for such a gentle stone. This is less surprising perhaps when you know that pink is the colour associated with Venus, the Roman goddess of love and desire. Amorous Venus rules passion and eroticism, love and affection, and Rose Quartz is tender and passionate, erotic and exciting.

Before undertaking any of the rituals in this book, the crystals should be purified, dedicated and programmed (see page 15) before use. It is traditional to bathe and wear clean clothes when working a ritual – pink or red depending on whether you want romance or red-hot passion. Burning a sweetgrass smudge stick (a bundle of herbs tied together especially for burning) or rose joss stick prepares the room and you can anoint yourself with rose oil. Pink candles set the scene and appropriate background music assists your concentration.

When carrying out rituals, consciously make your movements slow to focus the mind. During the 'Attracting love ritual' (see page 24), you should try to move with voluptuous intent.

SEEING LOVE

Seer stones have been used since the beginning of time to see into the future and Rose Quartz is attuned to Venus, the Roman love goddess. If you are looking for a lover, hold your Rose Quartz seer stone on the evening before Valentine's Day (or at any full moon) and take a deep slow breath, drawing peace and calm into your heart. Breathe out and say: 'Venus, goddess of love, please show me my true love in the stone.' Let your eyes go slightly out of focus and the image will form.

Seer stone

RITUAL: ATTRACTING LOVE

This ritual uses Rose Quartz and Danburite but you can substitute any of the love attracting crystals listed on page 20. The Danburite emphasizes the twin flame aspect of love. This crystal packs a powerful punch into a small piece. If you desire loving companionship, replace the Danburite with Sugilite, but if it's a hot date you want, replace the Danburite with lusty Ruby or fiery Garnet, powerful attractors of erotic love. Green Aventurine invites passion into the lives of those of more mature years.

If you already have a lover, rather than calling in your twin flame (see Step 3), ask that more love will manifest between the two of you and that the relationship becomes the best that it can be.

Most potent time: new moon.

You will need:
4 Rose Quartz crystals
l Danburite crystal
4 candles in candle holders made from Rose Quartz
a silk cloth

1. Place your crystals and four candles on a table covered with a silk cloth. Position one candle to the north, welcoming in love from that direction as you light it. Place one to the south, one to the east and one to the west, each time welcoming love from that direction. Ask that the light from these candles act as guardian and keep you safe, attracting the highest manifestation of love.

2. Take your Rose Quartz crystals in your hands and sit down facing your table (if the crystals are large, hold one at a time). Close your eyes and quietly attune to the crystals. Let their energy flow through your hands, up your arms and into your heart. As the energy reaches your heart, feel it open out and expand. Touch the crystals to your heart. Rose Quartz is a powerful heart cleanser and healer so allow your heart to be purified by the energies of the crystals. Say out loud:
'I am a magnet for love. I welcome love into my heart and love into my life.'

3. Place the crystals on the table and pick up the Danburite. Say out loud:
'I call on my twin flame to be present and to manifest fully and lovingly in my life.' [OR: 'I call on the love between my lover and myself to manifest fully and unconditionally, loving and supporting us both.']

4. Sit quietly for a few moments with your eyes focused on the crystals. Picture what your life is like when you have the deeply passionate and mutually supportive love of your twin flame at your side [or when you and your lover manifest all the love that is possible between you]. Send that picture out into the future, unrolling it before you so that you walk that path.

5. When you are ready to complete the ritual, get up and blow out each candle in turn saying:
'I send light and love into the world and it returns to me tenfold.'
Either leave the crystals on the table, or place them around your bed.

UNCONDITIONAL LOVE

Unconditional love is the best basis for relationships. Truly unconditional love shared by lovers is mutually supportive and trust-enhancing. There are many misconceptions about unconditional love. Yes, it is a love that loves someone 'warts and all', accepting them as they are without trying to force them to change, but it does not mean getting tangled up in their dramas and traumas, nor does it mean being emotionally abused.

Unconditional love is non-manipulative and non-coercive. It means seeing someone as the most wonderful person in the world (we all are!) and accepting that sometimes they may not behave as though they are, and that there is nothing you can do about that – it is up to them. Unconditional love means realizing that you are not responsible for someone else's actions or thoughts. It means standing placidly by, offering loving acceptance while someone sorts out their own life, not doing it for them. It also means saying: 'I love you and I am taking care of myself by staying in a good space within myself.'

Unconditional love sets boundaries. It certainly does not mean being walked all over, abused or any of the myriad forms of victimization or domination that sometimes pass for unconditional love. Sometimes the most loving thing you can do for someone – and for yourself – is to walk away.

WHICH CRYSTALS?

All crystals radiate unconditional love but certain crystals encourage you to love unconditionally. Wear Cymophane, soft pink Danburite or radiant Petalite on a long chain over your heart. A Selenite pillar or large chunk of Rose Quartz in your home ensures an abundant supply of unconditional love. Crystalline Kyanite is useful for smoothing the way for unconditional love in lasting relationships. Two stones are required – one for each person. The stones can be programmed to bring harmony and unconditional love to the partnership.

Additional crystals: Variscite, Rhodochrosite, Morganite, Kunzite, Cobalto-Calcite, Larimar.

Cymophane

Crystalline Kyanite

Selenite pillar

RITUAL: ATTRACTING UNCONDITIONAL LOVE

Giving and sharing unconditional love is a profoundly self-empowering experience that opens the heart to a truly loving life.

Most potent time: new moon.

You will need:
1 Selenite or Rose Quartz egg- or heart-shaped crystal

1. Sit holding your crystal and close your eyes. Feel the unconditional love radiating out from the crystal, moving up your arms, across your shoulders and down into your heart. Feel how the energy opens and warms your heart.

2. Put your crystal on your heart and feel the love go to deep within you. Allow a wave of that unconditional love to flow out to the world and then return to you. As it returns, it draws unconditional love towards you. Welcome the love into your heart and tell yourself that it is manifesting in the outer world at this very moment.

RITUAL: SHARING UNCONDITIONAL LOVE

When you have found your lover, sit facing each other in a softly lit room
– candlelight is ideal – and perform this ritual.

Most potent time: new moon (but beneficial at any time).

You will need:

2 Selenite or Rose Quartz egg- or heart-shaped crystals

1. Take a crystal each and sit facing
   each other. Cup your crystal in your
   hands and feel the unconditional love
   radiating out.

2. Now close your eyes for a few moments
   then open them and look deep into
   your lover's eyes, looking with the eyes
   of unconditional love.

3. Place your crystal over your lover's
   heart and hold it there while your lover
   puts their crystal to your heart. Keeping
   your eyes and hearts open, share the
   unconditional love between you. When
   you are ready, put the crystals down
   but allow the unconditional love to
   continue in your lives.

THE LOVE LAYOUT

Laying out stones creates an energetic grid around you, pulling in an abundance of love and transforming any negative feelings or expectations you may have. You don't have to use large stones – small tumbled ones are very effective. If your stones have points, place them pointing inwards to draw the energies towards you.

LAYOUT: LAYING OUT LOVE STONES

It's easiest to do this layout while lying on the floor, but you could lay one permanently around your bed, placing the stones under the mattress so that you enjoy the benefits every night.

If you are lying on the floor, make sure you are warm and comfortable and won't be disturbed. Place the stones on the floor around you in the order given below.

You will need:

1 Red Jasper crystal
2 Carnelian crystals
2 Smoky Quartz crystals
2 Danburite crystals
2 Rhodochrosite crystals
1 Dioptase (optional) crystal
2 Cobalto-Calcite crystals
1 Selenite crystal
1 Spirit or clear Quartz crystal

1. Place the Red Jasper beneath and between your feet to draw energy and love from the earth.

2. Place a Carnelian either side of your groin to energize your creative centres.

3. Lay a Smoky Quartz crystal either side of your hips to cleanse and energize and bring in universal love.

4. Lay Danburite either side of your solar plexus to draw in love and gently transform energy.

5. Place Rhodochrosite either side of your heart to bathe you in unconditional love and acceptance.

6. If using Dioptase, place it over the base of your breastbone to open the higher heart energies and draw universal love deep into your heart.

7. Lay Cobalto-Calcite either side of your throat to bring love into all your communications and joy into all you speak.

8. Place Selenite on your brow to bathe you in unconditional, universal love and help you see life through loving eyes.

9. Position Spirit or clear Quartz above your head, pointing down to draw in love from the highest spiritual realms and enfold you within the embrace of your guardian angel.

ACCENTUATING THE POSITIVE WITH CRYSTALS

Crystals can help you draw positive qualities into your relationships. As with all crystals, they work best when programmed specifically for that task (see page 15).

Ametrine

COMPATIBILITY

To attract a compatible lover or to enhance compatibility with a present lover, keep a tumbled Ametrine in your pocket. This will speedily bring you into accord. Large pieces of Ametrine are decorative and ensure harmony when placed in your home.

Additional crystals: Celestite, Merlinite, Chrysanthemum stone.

Diamond

FIDELITY

If you desire a faithful lover, gift yourself a diamond pendant and wear it over your heart. A Diamond is the ideal gift between lovers as it signifies fidelity. It brings love into a relationship and is a symbol of bonding and commitment.

Additional crystals: Chrysoprase, Green Sapphire, Blue Tourmaline.

Cobalto-Calcite

HOPE

Cobalto-Calcite instils hope in all who hold it. Place it over your heart to bring hope into the darkest of situations.

Additional crystals: Pink Tourmaline, Pink Topaz, Rhodochrosite, Blue Quartz, Moss Agate, Garnet, Variscite.

INDEPENDENCE

While it may seem paradoxical to find independence in a chapter on attracting love, being independent helps you to wait for the right love to come along and to enjoy your own company in the meantime. Sunstone helps you stand on your own two feet and to meet situations with confidence and an independent mind.

Additional crystals: Morganite, Jasper, Rhodonite, Cobalto-Calcite, Selenite, Candle Quartz, Tree Agate, Ocean Jasper, Blue Lace Agate, Green Tourmaline.

Sunstone

JOY

Topaz is a powerful bringer of joy. Nothing miserable survives around its sunny emanations for long and it uplifts your heart whenever you wear it.

Additional crystals: Orange Carnelian, Citrine, Watermelon Tourmaline, Youngite, Pink Crackle Quartz, Sunstone, Dendritic Agate, Morganite, Emerald, Muscovite, Opal Aura.

Topaz

Green Tourmaline

TENDERNESS

If you yearn for more tenderness in your life, place a Green Tourmaline or Larimar over your heart. This opens you to give and receive loving kindness and tender loving care. Watermelon Tourmaline, a combination of green and pink, will attract a tender lover into your life. Pink Crackle Quartz also encourages tenderness between lovers.

Additional crystals: Morganite, Pink Agate.

Watermelon Tourmaline

YOUR
SEX LIFE

crystals activate the subtle
sexual centres in your body

CRYSTAL APHRODISIACS

Crystals are powerful aphrodisiacs, activating the subtle sexual centres in your body, the base and the sacral chakras (see pages 82–85), so that erotic energy is highly charged, inhibitions are removed, and love is given and exchanged freely. Your sex life is greatly enhanced if you and your lover share a sexual recharge (see page 40), placing the stones on each other as part of foreplay or enfolding them between your bodies during lovemaking (use gently rounded tumbled stones for comfort). You can also use the sexual recharge to heighten your sex appeal before a night out. You will have an irresistible aura of love.

APHRODISIAC CRYSTALS

Aphrodisiac crystals work well when tucked under your pillow or placed around your living room or bedroom. An excellent way to enjoy them with your lover is to take a crystal love bath together – although you can also enjoy one alone and bathe yourself in love. Aphrodisiac crystals also make energizing gem essences (see page 16) for gently rubbing on the appropriate parts of your body.

Pink Tourmaline

If you desire to spice up your love life, or need a little help in the love department, look no further than Pink Tourmaline. This beautiful stone stimulates libido and encourages you to share physical pleasure with your lover. It is particularly effective made into a gem essence and rubbed on your wrists before bed.

Pink Tourmaline

Red Jasper

This is an excellent stone for stimulating libido and prolonging sexual pleasure. Red Jasper energizes and cleanses the sex organs and is particularly appropriate for men, although women benefit, too, and might like to try a Red Jasper love ball.

Red Jasper

Orange Carnelian

A recharging crystal, vibrant Orange Carnelian energizes the creative centres, overcomes impotence or frigidity, and restores vitality to the female sex organs.

Orange Carnelian

Smoky Quartz

If you have any hang-ups about sexual matters, Smoky Quartz helps you accept that sex is a normal, natural and highly enjoyable part of life. It enhances virility and cleanses the sexual centres so that your passion flows freely.

Smoky Quartz

Rose Quartz

Rose Quartz

By opening your heart centre, Rose Quartz restores love and trust between you and your lover. It teaches you how to love yourself and to receive love from someone else. It is also believed to increase fertility.

Red Garnet

Red Garnet

By promoting passion and increasing your sexual potency, Red Garnet revives and revitalizes your sex life.

Red-Black Mahogany

Red-Black Mahogany

Powerful Red-Black Mahogany increases virility and stamina, keeping you grounded in your body so that sex becomes a full-body experience.

Variscite

Variscite

A useful crystal if you or your lover's interest in sex wanes, Variscite restores libido, increases sexual energy and helps bring more unconditional love into the situation.

Pietersite

Pietersite

The perfect stone for when old vows of celibacy have been holding you back, Pietersite resolves your internal conflicts and increases your stamina.

VIRILITY CRYSTALS

Virility is an attitude of mind and a product of your feelings.
If you feel potent and sexually powerful, and believe you can
express this with both passion and tenderness, your virility will
increase. You do not have to be excessively macho to be virile,
strength is an inner quality that resonates with the gentle power
of crystals.

Smoky Quartz

This is an excellent stone for improving virility. Place it over
the base and sacral chakras (see pages 82–85) to cleanse and
energize them, or rub the gem essence over your belly. You can
also use a Smoky Quartz wand to massage your lover and
prolong mutual pleasure.

Smoky Quartz

Red Jasper

This is the stone to wear if you desire an uninhibited night of
passion. It encourages sex that goes on – and on. Try giving
your lover a belly massage by moving a rounded stone in ever
increasing circles. It will drive your lover wild.

Additional crystals: Red-Black Obsidian, Carnelian, Zircon.

Red Jasper

RITUAL: THE SEXUAL RECHARGE

Half an hour with the recharge crystals fires up your sexual energy and puts you in the mood for love. It's excellent before going out clubbing or partying – prospective lovers won't be able to resist. You can share the recharge, too. It's a perfect holiday activity on a secluded beach with warm sand and gently lapping waves, or in the privacy of your hotel room on a hot sleepy afternoon, but you can enjoy it anywhere you can get up close and personal with your lover.

Most potent time: before a hot date (but the light of the full moon works especially well, or under a tropical sun).

You will need:

1 Rose Quartz crystal
1 Smoky Quartz crystal
1 Red Jasper crystal
1 Orange Carnelian crystal

1. Lie on your bed or in a warm place where you will not be disturbed. If you are doing the recharge with a lover, lie close together and place stones on each other in turn or lay them between your bodies if lying one on top of the other. If you're giving yourself a recharge, have all the crystals close at hand.

2. Gently massage the area above your heart and place a Rose Quartz on your heart to open it to receive love.

3. Gently massage the inside of your thighs and place Smoky Quartz between your thighs so that your passion can flow freely.

4. Gently massage the area around your pubic bone and place Red Jasper at the base of your pubic bone to stimulate your libido and energize the base chakra. This fiery stone prolongs sexual pleasure.

5. Gently massage the area just below your navel and place Orange Carnelian on your sacral chakra to recharge it and open your creative energy.

6. Leave the stones in place for 10–15 minutes so that you absorb the energy. If you are with a lover, breathe in unison and gaze into each other's eyes.

INTIMACY AND LOVING COMMUNICATION

Intimacy enhances your sex life. The soft flakes of Muscovite open your heart to intimate sharing, while Hemimorphite encourages open and honest emotional communication, allowing you to say exactly how you feel. Carry one with you when you ask out that divine person you've been eyeing for a date. They won't be able to resist.

Pink Kunzite

Sugilite

To encourage loving communication between yourself and a prospective lover, carry a piece of Kunzite or Crystalline Kyanite. Hold one whenever you need to have a frank discussion. **Additional crystals:** Lapis Lazuli, Turquoise, Blue Lace Agate, Strombolite.

UNDERSTANDING EACH OTHER

If you have difficulty communicating your desires, feel that your lover does not understand you, or want to understand someone else better, seek the help of Sugilite. This stone brings light into the darkest of misunderstandings. It is beneficial for two people to carry similar-sized stones that have been magnetized to their twin (see ritual opposite). If you are developing a relationship, it is also effective to meditate together for 10 minutes morning and evening, each holding a Sugilite and focusing on opening communication between your hearts. Alternatively, if your partner is too shy to participate in a ritual, perhaps you could slip a Sugilite into their pocket and let it work quietly.

RITUAL: ENHANCING MUTUAL UNDERSTANDING

In this ritual, which requires two participants, two Sugilite stones are magnetized to each other. Carrying one of these stones each will help two people understand each other better.

Most potent time: the day before full moon.

You will need:
2 Sugilite crystals

1. Place the two Sugilite crystals in sunlight together, preferably on a day that will be followed by the light of the full moon. Say together:
   'We magnetize these two stones and dedicate them to enhancing our understanding of each other.'

2. Leave the stones in place until the next morning and then each of you should carry one in your pocket. Every time you handle the stone, think of your lover and grow in understanding.

LOVE STONES

When choosing jewellery for yourself, or looking for a love gift, select a stone that resonates astrologically. This heightens your sexual energy and adds new vitality to your love life – or to that of a friend. (See Directory, pages 108–125 for the qualities of the stones.)

BIRTHSTONES BY ASTROLOGICAL SIGN

Sign	Glyph	Birthstone(s)
Aries	♈	Ruby, Diamond
Taurus	♉	Emerald
Gemini	♊	Agate, Tourmaline
Cancer	♋	Moonstone, Pearl
Leo	♌	Cat's or Tiger's Eye
Virgo	♍	Peridot, Sardonyx
Libra	♎	Sapphire, Opal
Scorpio	♏	Malachite, Turquoise
Sagittarius	♐	Topaz, Turquoise, Tanzanite
Capricorn	♑	Onyx, Garnet
Aquarius	♒	Aquamarine
Pisces	♓	Amethyst

Amethyst

Diamond

Garnet

Aquamarine

Emerald

Pearl

BIRTHSTONES BY MONTH

Month	Birthstone(s)
January	Garnet
February	Amethyst
March	Aquamarine
April	Diamond
May	Emerald
June	Pearl, Moonstone
July	Ruby
August	Peridot
September	Sapphire
October	Opal
November	Topaz
December	Turquoise, Tanzanite

Ruby

Peridot

Sapphire

Opal

Topaz

Turquoise

CRYSTALS FOR SEXUAL PROBLEMS

Hidden causes sometimes create problems, such as impotence, frigidity, premature ejaculation or crippling inhibitions, but crystals reverse them. Crystals can also help you to rekindle love.

RITUAL: HEALING SEXUAL PROBLEMS

The swirling whorls of powerful Malachite, a stone long prized for its ability to draw off toxic emotions, assist if you feel frigid or inhibited.

Most potent time: full moon.

You will need:

1 Malachite crystal

1. Sit quietly holding the Malachite and allow yourself to relax. Follow its bands inward with your eyes until you reach the source of your problems. Do not try to force them, simply let them float up into your awareness, and allow the power of Malachite to draw out the old trauma and release it into the stone. Repeat: *'I let go, I release, I heal.'*

2. You may need to follow this up with appropriate crystals or with a ritual to heal abuse (see page 74). You can also tape Malachite over your solar plexus at night. Before you sleep, tell yourself that dreams will show you the cause of your difficulty and transform it, the stone drawing off the pain and freeing you from the past. You may need to follow this up the next day with a 'love stone' such as Rhodonite or Rose Quartz, to further heal your heart, or a Yellow Jasper on your solar plexus to re-energize your emotional centre.

INFIDELITY

Emerald has long been known as the 'stone of successful love' as it induces domestic bliss and keeps a relationship in balance. There are times, however, when it is beyond the power of even an Emerald to hold a relationship together. If this stone changes colour it is said to warn of unfaithfulness. If you suspect a male lover may be straying, gift him a Turquoise. It, too, changes colour when there is a danger of infidelity. If a female lover is the object of suspicion, try the age-old test of placing a piece of Magnetite under her pillow. If she falls out of bed during the night or calls out a name that is not yours, your suspicions are confirmed.

Emerald

Magnetite

However, suspicion is not beneficial to relationships. It would be better to use restoring trust stones to help you replace suspicion with trust – your lover is sure to repay you with faithfulness. Repeat the 'Trust affirmation' each morning, looking into your eyes in a mirror while holding a restoring trust stone.

On the other hand, it may well be time to recognize that a relationship has come to its natural end and that it is time to move on. In which case, choose stones that support your strength and encourage moving on, such as Rainbow Obsidian (see 'Letting go of old love', page 56). **Trust affirmation:** 'I am loving, I am trusting, I open my heart to trust.'

Restoring trust crystals: Garnet, Rhodonite, Kunzite, Rose Quartz, Pink or Watermelon Tourmaline.

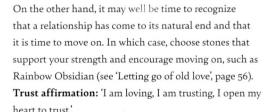

Garnet

REKINDLING LOVE

If you are in a partnership that is feeling a bit jaded, the bright energies of Beryl rekindle love, especially in its beautiful pink Morganite form. Wear it, rub the gem essence over your heart or place one under your pillow or in your bedroom where both partners can see it from the bed.

Morganite

Additional crystals: Morganite, Diamond, Tourmalinated Quartz, Mangano Calcite, Larimar.

Turquoise

INHIBITIONS

Turquoise, Pink Crackle Quartz and Garnets are excellent crystals for helping you to shed your inhibitions. Deck yourself in Turquoise or Garnet jewellery before a date, or place a large piece of Crackle Quartz by your bed. Despite its delicate nature, opal has always been prized as an engagement ring – perhaps because it, too, is an inhibition-releaser. The 'Feeling safe' affirmation (page 50) helps you to shed your inhibitions.
Uninhibited affirmation: 'I am free to express myself, I let myself go fully and enjoy my body and its wonderful erotic sensations.'
Additional crystals: Malachite, Sunstone.

PREMATURE EJACULATION

Rutilated Quartz

Rutilated Quartz has been used for centuries to slow down premature ejaculation and to find the cause that underlies it. Tape the stone on the sacral chakra and a Red Jasper on the base chakra (see pages 82–85) and ask for a healing dream that reveals and transmutes the underlying fear.

Slowing down ejaculation affirmation: 'I am safe, there's plenty of time, I slow things down and take my time. I have all the time in the world.'

FRIGIDITY

Frigidity occurs when you can't relax enough to trust your lover and allow true intimacy between you. Gem essences are particularly effective. Make a combined essence (see page 16) from Red Jasper, Carnelian and Rose Quartz (add a Uvarovite Garnet if you have one). Rub a few drops on your belly, morning and night for several weeks. Then, holding the crystals, stand with your feet slightly apart and push your hips out to the left, then circle backwards, out to the right and forwards so that your hips trace a large circle. Repeat 10 times and then 10 times in the other direction.

You can also place 'feeling safe' crystals under your mattress or tape them over your belly at night. Repeat the 'Feeling safe affirmation' every morning and night while looking into your eyes in a mirror and holding a 'feeling safe' stone.

Red Jasper

Carnelian

Rose Quartz

Feeling safe affirmation: 'I am safe, I am loved, it is safe to allow myself to love and be loved fully and intimately.'
Feeling safe crystals: Rose Quartz, Rhodochrosite, Carnelian, Selenite, Pietersite, Aventurine.

IMPOTENCE

Impotence is often connected with a lack of vital life force and vitality that can be restored using crystals but it may have deep psychological causes ascertainable by dowsing and treating with appropriate crystals (see 'Transforming distressing feelings with crystals', page 66).

Shiva Lingam

The fiery red of Red Carnelian or Red Jasper re-energizes the base chakra and removes blockages. It ensures a good blood supply to vital organs. Either place it over the base and sacral chakras (see pages 82–85) or rub a gem essence (see page 16) made from a combination of these stones and Rutilated Quartz over the lower chakras and sex organs for several weeks. A Shiva Lingam works by the principle of sympathetic magic, an ancient belief that something that looks like what you are trying to achieve will bring it about. Thus, a Shiva Lingam, which looks like an erect phallus, has been used for hundreds of years to heal impotence – keep one in a trouser pocket or under a pillow.

Amazonite

Potency affirmation: 'I am potent, I am creative, I am filled with vital force and energy.'
Additional crystals: Amazonite, Morganite, Ruby, Variscite.

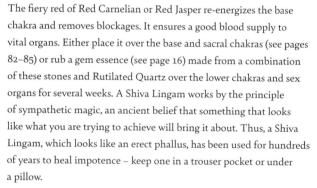

CRYSTAL LOVE BATHING

Being bathed in love is a wonderful experience. The crystal love bath is erotic and romantic when taken with a lover but you can also take one alone, absorbing the loving emanations of the crystals into yourself and treating yourself to full body love.

RITUAL: CRYSTAL LOVE BATH

To take a crystal love bath, first prepare the room carefully, cleaning it and dedicating it to love. Use rose-scented candles since rose is traditionally the scent of love and, for the bath, choose rounded pieces of Rose Quartz for sensual comfort.

Most potent time: any time.

You will need:

1 or 2 Danburite or Larimar crystals
several largish pieces of Rose Quartz
rose-scented candles in candle holders made from Rose Quartz
rose oil
Rose Quartz or Ruby gem essence (optional)

1. Place rose-scented candles around the room and place one or two pieces of Danburite or Larimar at each end of the bath. Place the Rose Quartz in the bath before running the water. You can add other crystals to the water but do ensure that they won't dissolve or fragment (see Directory, pages 108–125). Delicate crystals are best placed around the bath. If you have some Rose Quartz gem essence add several drops to the bath water. Spritz the room, too, if you like – add Ruby for passion if you are with your lover.

2. When you are ready, immerse yourself in the water. Lie back, close your eyes and breathe deeply. Feel the crystal water vibrating gently and infusing your body with love. Massage the area around your heart and your belly. Stay in the crystal bath as long as possible to enjoy whole body love.

BREAKING PAST TIES

---

crystals help you let go of
old love and move on

LETTING GO OF OLD LOVE

Old love affairs often interfere with new ones, even when they are long over. If a lover has left you and you are having difficulty getting over it, wear beautiful Rainbow Obsidian over your heart. This gentle stone severs the cords of old love, encouraging letting go and moving on. It helps you appreciate the positive aspect of your experience, recognizing the lessons you have learned and the strengths and qualities you developed during the course of the relationship.

The 'Letting go affirmation' helps you to move on, repeat it three or four times a day while holding Rainbow Obsidian over your heart until you no longer feel you need it.
Letting go affirmation: 'I let go of anyone and everyone in my life that I am holding on to who is no longer appropriate. I set myself free. I am independent and whole in myself.'

RITUAL: PULVERIZING BONDS THAT BIND YOUR HEART

Unbeknown to you, you may be tied by heart cords to an old love you haven't fully let go of yet, or need to free yourself from a recent lover. You may be tied to someone from the past you have forgotten all about, or even – if you believe in reincarnation – to someone from another life perhaps. This ritual frees you. It is important that you see the heart as representing the *cords* that bind you, not the other person.
Most potent time: full moon.

You will need:

thin heart of crystal, such as Jasper
cloth or newspaper
gloves
eye shield
large hammer

1. Wrap the crystal heart in cloth or newspaper to avoid injury from flying shards then
   place on a hard surface. Wearing gloves and an eye shield, pick up the hammer, hold
   it high and say out loud:
   *'I now release my heart from any bonds, cords or ties that bind it from whenever and
   wherever they may have arisen. I set myself and my heart free.'*

2. Bring the hammer down with force on to the crystal. Continue hammering until the
   crystal is shattered into dust.

3. Gather up the dust and sprinkle
   it around a plant to fertilize new
   growth. Feel how free your heart now
   is, how light.

4. Follow up this ritual by placing a
   gentle heart healer, such as Rose
   Quartz or Rhodochrosite, over your
   own heart and allowing the energy to
   replenish the love within your heart.

CUTTING THE BONDS

Cutting bonds is an excellent method of freeing yourself from an old love, especially where the past has been holding you back from loving again. Surprisingly, it also works very well with a present lover, too, as it does not cut off any unconditional love between you. Rather it clears away all the expectations, obligations, karma (baggage from the past – from this or any other life) and intentions that have built up and which get in the way of unconditional loving.

If you don't have a photograph of the person with whom you are cutting the bonds, draw the outline of a man/woman on paper and write the person's name on it.
Most potent time: full moon.

You will need:

1 Botswana or Banded Agate crystal

1 Rose Quartz crystal

1 Smoky Quartz crystal

photograph of the person concerned or named person drawn on

a piece of paper

1. Using the photograph or drawn outline, gently outline the person with your Agate. As you do so, picture all the bonds and expectations that tie you together falling away, other than an unconditionally loving heart connection if you wish.

2. Then work up each chakra in turn, circling it with the crystal and again picturing the bonds falling away. Gently rotate the Agate over the chakras of your own body, picturing the bonds falling away.

3. When you have completed this, place the Rose Quartz on the person's heart and feel unconditional love and forgiveness radiating out from the crystal into both your hearts. Leave the crystal on the photograph or drawing.

4. Take the Smoky Quartz and pass it around the photograph or drawing and all around yourself, allowing it to absorb all the bonds and transmute them into pure loving energy that radiates out to you both.

RELEASING A VOW OR PROMISE

It is surprising just how much the things you say can tie you to someone, or affect your freedom to love. If you have made vows in the past that are interfering with your ability to form relationships in the present, or which are inappropriately tying you to people from your past, the vows can be reframed with the assistance of crystals. Typical vows include celibacy from a previous life as a monk or nun, or a promise to someone that pulls you back into a relationship across time. Such promises include: 'I'll always look after you', 'I'll always love you', 'I'll always be there for you' and so on – usually made without realizing quite how long eternity is. Fortunately you do not always need to know what the promise or vow was, or when it was made. But if you have made a vow in your present life – such as 'I'll always love you' or 'till death us do part', it can be very beneficial to specifically free yourself from that vow.

Most potent time: full moon.

You will need:
1 Pietersite, Blue Lace or Banded Agate, or Brandenberg crystal

1. Holding your crystal in your hands, relax and close your eyes. Bring your awareness into the crystal in your hands. Say out loud:

    'I use the power of this crystal to release me from any vow, promise or soul contract that no longer serves me, no matter when or to whom it was made. I set myself free.'
    (If you are aware of any vow – such as a previous marriage vow – that is no longer serving or appropriate for you, be specific and state that this particular vow no longer binds you.)

2. Put down the crystal and clap your hands loudly, saying as you do so: *'So be it.'*

HEALING HEARTBREAK

Broken hearts can take a long time to mend and wounds to the heart make you cautious about trying love again. Heartache creates a barrier to intimacy and trust. This pain can be healed with softly banded Rhodochrosite, the heart healer par excellence.

Rhodochrosite helps you to assimilate painful feelings without shutting down your heart, and boosts how you feel about yourself. To heal heartache, wear this gentle crystal as a pendant over your heart for several weeks or rub the gem essence over your breastbone two or three times a day. The stone can also be taped in place overnight. Repeat the 'Whole heart affirmation' out loud several times a day for a few days after the ritual. **Whole heart affirmation:** 'My heart is healed, my heart is whole, my heart is filled with love.'

HEART-HEALERS

The following crystals are all good alternatives to Rhodochrosite and can be used in the same way – worn over the heart as jewellery or taped in place, or used as a gem essence rubbed over the breastbone.

Agate

Agate

Strong but slow working, Agate heals bitterness of the heart. It is particularly useful when heartbreak is deeply entrenched and accompanied by resentment or a sense of having been betrayed. It gives you the courage to start again.

Rainbow Obsidian

Beautiful banded Rainbow Obsidian gently releases past pain, cuts the cords of old love, removes hooks that others have left in your heart, and clears emotional bondage. You may need to wear it for several weeks to complete the healing process.

Rainbow Obsidian

Kunzite

Pink Kunzite is an excellent healer for depression following the break-up of a relationship. If your heart is full of emotional debris, tranquil Pink Kunzite dissolves it and brings in unconditional love to heal your heart.

Pink Kunzite

Rhodonite

Powerful Rhodonite is a useful first aid measure when your heart is first broken, and an emotional balancer that brings your heart back online. It is helpful when you have been betrayed and are set on revenge or self-destruction, as it ameliorates these feelings.

Rhodonite

Larimar

Soft and gentle Larimar restores playfulness and childlike joy and is therefore the ideal stone for healing a broken heart or other trauma that may have closed down the heart.

Additional crystals: Rose Quartz, Dioptase, Pink Tourmaline, Morganite.

Larimar

RITUAL: HEALING HEARTBREAK

This ritual uses the power of visualization and affirmation. Visualization is literally seeing pictures in your mind's eye but you can use a photograph to assist. Affirmation is saying something that you want to occur *as though it is happening in the present.* When you affirm something, you bring it into being.

Most potent time: full moon.

You will need:

1 Rhodochrosite crystal
a pink candle in a candle holder made from Rose Quartz
photograph of the person concerned (optional)

1. Choose a time when you will not be disturbed and find a place where you feel happy and at home – a place outside perhaps or a favourite room. Settle yourself comfortably, light the candle and close your eyes.

2. In your mind's eye, picture yourself facing the person who created your heartbreak [if you find this difficult, open your eyes and look at a photograph]. Allow yourself to fully feel the pain of that parting and the heartbreak that followed. Honour your feelings. In your mind, tell the other person how it made you feel. Say whatever you need to say – get it all out and do not hold back.

3. Pick up the Rhodochrosite and hold it to your heart. Feel the loving and forgiving energies of the stone enfold your heart, offering you healing. Picture the broken shards of your heart knitting together again so that it is whole and freed from the pain. Say out loud:
   'My heart is healed, my heart is whole, my heart is my own.'

4. Keep the stone in place. Now think about the person again and send the loving and forgiving pink energy of the Rhodochrosite to the other person. Say out loud:
'I forgive you, I let you go.'

5. Picture the other person turning and walking away from you, let them go with unconditional love and forgiveness. Blow out the candle.

6. Come back to yourself, feel the energy of the stone on your heart once again. Feel how loving and forgiving it is, how it enfolds you within its rosettes, wrapping you in unconditional love. Say out loud:
'My heart is healed, my heart is whole, my heart is filled with love.'

7. Keep the stone with you to remind you that your heart is now healed.

Rhodochrosite

TRANSFORMING DISTRESSING FEELINGS WITH CRYSTALS

Feelings such as neediness or a fear that you will never find love are offputting to other people, who pick up on them without realizing. These feelings, along with others such as having been abandoned or abused, can stand in the way of finding true love but can easily be transformed with crystals.

To find the crystal you need, dowse (see page 12) the list of crystals below, asking which is most beneficial for you to clear the distressing feelings at this time. When you have found the right crystal for you, hold it or place it over the appropriate chakra on your body (see below and pages 82–85). You will then experience the positive effect associated with that crystal.

Rose Quartz

Abandonment and Rejection

Rose Quartz is an excellent stone for healing feelings of abandonment and rejection, reconnecting you to a source of deep love, self-acceptance and healing.

Additional crystals: Rhodochrosite, Peach Selenite, Pink Phantom Quartz, Lavender-Pink Smithsonite, Dioptase, Sunstone, Blue Lace Agate, Pink Sapphire. **Chakra:** base, heart, past life. **Positive feelings:** accepted and loved.

Abuse

Pink Crackle Quartz is a versatile stone, healing emotional and physical abuse and bringing in bright nurturing energy. Youngite heals your inner child and Larimar restores playfulness and childlike innocence. (See also page 74.)
Additional crystals: Smoky Rose Quartz, Shiva Lingam, Rhodochrosite, Pink Agate, Pink Carnelian, Blue Lace Agate, Ruby Aura Quartz, Pink Sapphire, Lavender-Pink Smithsonite. **Chakra:** base, sacral.
Positive feelings: nurtured and loved.

Pink Crackle Quartz

Aggression and Anger

If you feel angry all the time you will feel prickly with other people, but Carnelian carried in your pocket absorbs anger and frustration.
Additional crystals: Rose Quartz, Ruby Aura Quartz, Bloodstone, Amethyst, Rose Quartz, Ruby, Blue Lace Agate, Amethyst, Muscovite, Peridot, Blue-Green Smithsonite. **Chakra:** base. **Positive feelings:** good humoured and peaceful.

Carnelian

Anxiety and Panic

Kunzite contains lithium, a natural tranquillizer, and it is the perfect calming stone to hold in your hand.
Additional crystals: Rose Quartz, Halite, Aventurine, Blue Phantom Quartz, Pink Crackle Quartz, Tanzanite, Emerald, Moonstone, Rutilated Quartz, Tiger's Eye, Tourmaline, Pink Sapphire. **Chakra:** earth, base, solar plexus, heart. **Positive feelings:** serene and carefree.

Kunzite

Apathy

If you feel that you just can't be bothered, Red Jasper soon gets you motivated. **Additional crystals:** Red Calcite. **Chakra:** base, sacral.
Positive feelings: energetic and involved.

Red Jasper

Rhodonite

Dependency and Co-dependency

If you've always leant on other people, Rhodonite encourages you to stand on your own feet and take responsibility for yourself.

Additional crystals: Sunstone, Lepidolite, Blue-Green Smithsonite. **Chakra:** base, solar plexus, heart. **Positive feelings:** independent and capable.

Ametrine

Depression, Despair and Despondency

Ametrine is a quick-acting antidepressant that brings sunshine and joy back into your life.

Additional crystals: Carnelian, Smoky Quartz, Tanzanite, Banded Agate, Blue Quartz, Kunzite, Sunstone, Botswana Agate, Lapis Lazuli, Moss Agate, Rutilated Quartz, Garnet, Tiger's Eye, Hematite, Purple Tourmaline, Pink Sapphire. **Chakra:** solar plexus. **Positive feelings:** joyous and hopeful.

Rose Quartz

Fear

Rose Quartz imparts deep strength that enables you to face down fear. For fear of failure use Hematite, for fear of responsibility use Citrine.

Additional crystals: Elestial Quartz, Rutilated Quartz, Emerald, Pink Sapphire, Blue-Green Smithsonite, Larimar. **Chakra:** heart, solar plexus. **Positive feelings:** fearless and trusting.

Rhodochrosite

Grief and Sadness

An excellent healer of grief, Rhodochrosite offers comfort and self-reliance.

Additional crystals: Mangano Calcite, Cobalto-Calcite, Red Jasper, Obsidian, Lapis Lazuli, Pink Sapphire. **Chakra:** heart, higher heart. **Positive feelings:** joyous.

Guilt

Rose Quartz restores a feeling of innocence and trust.
Additional crystals: Peridot, Jasper, Larimar. **Chakra:** solar plexus, higher heart. **Positive feelings:** innocent and guiltless.

Rutilated Quartz

Hatred

Rutilated Quartz's gentle energies overcome hatred and draw down love.
Additional crystals: Rose Quartz, Rhodochrosite, Blue-Green Smithsonite. **Chakra:** heart, solar plexus. **Positive feelings:** accepted and loved.

Diamond

Inability to Commit

Diamond is the ultimate symbol of commitment.
Additional crystals: Garnet, Tiger's Eye, Onyx. **Chakra:** heart.
Positive feelings: committed and certain.

Inadequacy, Inferiority and Insecurity

A powerful emotional cleanser, Yellow Jasper dissolves feelings of inferiority and helps you recognize your strengths.
Additional crystals: Garnet, Pink Sapphire, Lavender-Pink Smithsonite. **Chakra:** solar plexus. **Positive feelings:** capable and secure.

Yellow Jasper

Intolerance and Prejudice

Prejudice can get in the way of seeing the right lover for you.
If you suffer from prejudice, Magnesite helps you feel more loving and accepting.
Additional crystals: Zircon. **Chakra:** base, heart.
Positive feelings: accepted and loved.

Magnesite

Peridot

Jealousy

Peridot is an age-old remedy for jealousy, wear it constantly.
Additional crystals: Rhodochrosite, Amethyst. **Chakra:** heart.
Positive feelings: trusting.

Feeling Manipulated

Manipulation is a form of control. If you are manipulated, or manipulate other people, Pink Carnelian releases you and frees you to love.
Additional crystals: Petalite. **Chakra:** sacral, solar plexus, brow.
Positive feelings: accepted and safe.

Pink Carnelian

Negativity

Smoky Quartz is the stone *par excellence* for dissolving and absorbing negativity of any kind.
Additional crystals: Topaz, Carnelian, Smoky Elestial, Green Phantom Quartz, Pink Sapphire, Pink Halite, Black Kyanite. **Chakra:** earth, base, solar plexus, brow. **Positive feelings:** positive and optimistic.

Smoky Quartz

Repression

If you have been repressing your feelings, Rhodonite brings them to the surface for release.
Additional crystals: Lapis Lazuli, Youngite, Phantom Quartz.
Chakra: base, sacral. **Positive feelings:** expressive and free.

Rhodonite

Resentment

Rhodonite dissolves resentment and draws in positive, encouraging energy.
Additional crystals: Peridot, Rainbow Aura Quartz, Carnelian, Pink Sapphire.
Chakra: past life, base, heart. **Positive feelings:** joyous and welcoming.

Self-sabotage

Self-sabotage occurs when, despite good intentions, you somehow do something that causes your relationships to fail or puts someone off. Scapolite overcomes sabotaging yourself and enhances your efforts to have positive relationships, as does Tourmalinated Quartz and Larimar. **Additional crystals:** none available. **Chakra:** past life, solar plexus. **Positive feelings:** confident and self-assured.

Tourmalinated Quartz

Selfishness

Rose Quartz helps you to overcome selfishness, teaching you to have an open and generous heart. **Additional crystals:** Rhodonite. **Chakra:** heart. **Positive feelings:** unselfish and caring.

Rose Quartz

Stubbornness

If you need to become more adaptable, Pietersite transforms stubbornness and helps you adapt to change. **Additional crystals:** Mookaite Jasper. **Chakra:** base, solar plexus. **Positive feelings:** flexible and adaptive.

Pietersite

Victim Mentality and Martyrdom

Lapis Lazuli quickly transforms someone from being a victim into someone who is in control of life. **Additional crystals:** Tourmaline, Snow Quartz, Golden Beryl, Larimar. **Chakra:** past life, heart, solar plexus, base. **Positive feelings:** self-responsible and autonomous.

Lapis Lazuli

HEALING ABUSE WITH CRYSTALS

Abuse creates inner scars that interfere with your ability to enjoy truly loving relationships. Such abuse is not always physical. Many people don't realize that constant criticism is abusive, for instance. Self-confidence is destroyed, as is the ability to trust and let yourself go sufficiently to reach orgasm – or to allow someone to love you. Fortunately, the loving energies of crystals gently release the scars.

Inappropriate touching or tickling from adults, siblings or friends, is also abusive. Loving yourself wholeheartedly and unconditionally is the best healing gift you can give yourself, as is accepting yourself and your body as you are now. Whether the abuse was physical, emotional or mental, touching and pleasuring your body yourself with a loving crystal reprogrammes your body to enjoy sexual touch and helps you to feel safe, especially if you use a gently rounded Shiva Lingam. If you have a lover, after the initial healing has taken place repeat the ritual with your lover gently caressing your body with the crystal.

Shiva Lingam

Crystals for physical abuse:

Shiva Lingam, Pink Agate, Rhodonite, Rhodochrosite,
Pink Carnelian, Lavender-Pink or Blue-Green Smithsonite.
Chakra: base, sacral.

Pink Agate

Crystals for emotional abuse:

Rhodochrosite, Rhodonite, Rose Quartz, Pink Sapphire,
Blue-Green or Yellow Smithsonite.
Chakra: solar plexus, heart.

Pink Sapphire

Crystals for mental or verbal abuse:

Citrine, Kunzite, Tiger's Eye, Pietersite, Blue Lace Agate.
Chakra: throat, third eye, crown.

Pink Kunzite

RITUAL: HEALING ABUSE

This ritual is a form of self-love that brings about profound changes. Choose a tumbled or round-ended stone that you feel attracted to, or one that is effective for an abuse scar you carry. Make a gem essence from the stone (see page 16) before starting the ritual and, after the ritual is complete, follow it up by rubbing the essence on the appropriate chakras (see pages 82–85) for a week or two afterwards, or place the stone on the chakras twice a day.

Prepare carefully for the ritual. Have a long relaxing bath – you may like to do the ritual in your bath. Have the room warm and cosy, and ensure that you will not be disturbed. Being naked or wearing a loose robe facilitates the ritual, as does performing it at a full moon.

Most potent time: full moon.

You will need:
1 crystal for healing abuse (see page 72)
candles and candleholders

1. Light some candles. When you are comfortably settled, repeat the following feeling safe affirmation to yourself three times:
   'I am safe, I am loved, I trust myself.'

2. Take your crystal and hold it in your hands, telling yourself that the crystal helps you heal. Feel the loving energy of the crystal warming your hands and passing through your body. Remind yourself that your crystal is helping you to create a safe healing space and that it wishes you only good.

3. When you feel ready, gently stroke the crystal all over your body – you may like to begin with your hands or feet. Use circular massage movements or sweeping strokes, whatever feels comfortable and pleasurable for y our body.

4. Use the crystal to explore your body fully. Take your time and if anywhere feels the least uncomfortable, lay the crystal gently on that part and allow the healing energies of the crystal to make it feel good and safe. Recommence stroking and massaging your body with the crystal until your whole body is glowing with the pleasure of love.

CRYSTALS FOR EMOTIONAL TRANSFORMATION

crystals change negative behaviour
and thoughts into positive feelings

BLESSINGS JOURNAL

Counting your blessings has long been recognized as a way to multiply them – and to keep you focused on the positive side of your life. It highlights the gift in any situation, no matter how negative it may seem at the time. Keeping a blessings journal is a powerful way to reinforce your blessings and to remind you to show thankfulness for them.

STARTING OUT

You will need a pretty journal with handmade paper perhaps, or a leather-bound book that feels good to hold. You could glue flat crystals on to the cover – choose crystals that reinforce and multiply the blessings, or that bring blessings you wish to have. You could pick a silver, gold or purple pen for writing, something different to what you use everyday, to make the journal special.

New moon is an excellent time to begin. Make a title page: 'My Blessings'. Write a list of all the things you feel thankful for or blessed by. Begin each sentence: 'I feel thankful for...', 'I am happy that...' or 'I am blessed by...' as this strengthens your positive emotions and feeling of being blessed each time you write.

When you have run out of blessings, hold one of the blessings crystals listed below and think about the apparently negative love situations in your life and focus on what you learned from them. You may have been dumped by a boyfriend, for instance, only to find a much nicer person afterwards. Or you may have found that you actually liked living in solitude and taking time to get to know and like yourself – this is a potent blessing. Peridot is an extremely useful stone for helping you to see the blessing in all things.

Each night take a few moments to hold your blessings crystal, count your blessings and write them in your journal. Whenever you feel down, read your journal and see how blessed you are. If your journal does not have crystals on the cover, you could keep a large Spirit Quartz on or alongside it to multiply the blessings and radiate them out into your environment.

Blessings crystals: Amethyst, Peridot, Clear or Citrine Spirit Quartz, Rose Quartz, Morganite, Mangano Calcite, Elestial Quartz, Lavender Quartz, Muscovite, Strombolite, Larimar.

TRANSFORMING EMOTIONS WITH CRYSTALS

Have you sought love for so long and never found it, or found it only to lose it again – and again? If so, you are probably stuck in a pattern of negative expectation and wearing a Pink Sapphire could be the answer. Hidden feelings and your past experiences have a profound effect on your love life. They trip you up and are why things may not go as well as you hope when a new romance comes along. You could be endlessly repeating an ingrained pattern or carrying emotional baggage from the past but this can be put down quite easily.

Pink Sapphire

Transforming yourself by eliminating emotional blockages to intimacy, forgiving yourself and others, releasing distressing feelings, and changing how you view the past make an enormous difference to your love life. A most effective way of doing this is through chakra crystal healing (see pages 82–85), or by wearing an appropriate crystal over your heart.

CRYSTALS FOR EMOTIONAL HEALING

Rose Quartz is a master emotional healer, quickly bringing emotions into balance and smoothing the highs and lows of love. It gently brings out repressed or unexpressed emotions and offers you loving forgiveness. Carry it with you when you are distressed or perturbed.

Halite is an excellent general emotional healer and cleanser, as is Smoky Quartz. Place one in your bath or hang it beneath the showerhead. Halite slowly dissolves and washes away emotional debris but Smoky Quartz remains intact and should be purified and recharged regularly (see page 14). To reprogramme your emotions while you sleep, tape Yellow Smithsonite over your solar plexus or grid it around each corner of your bed. Wear crystals such as Rose Quartz or Pink Sapphire for continuous emotional healing until the feeling has dissipated (usually about a week).

Halite

EMOTIONAL 'RESCUE REMEDY'

Place a Rose Quartz over your heart, a Smoky Quartz over your solar plexus and an Amethyst over your higher heart chakra and leave in place for 20 minutes to restore emotional equilibrium. Alternatively, make a gem essence with all three crystals and rub the remedy essence over your wrist and heart when needed.

CHAKRA CRYSTAL HEALING

Effective points for emotional healing, the chakras are subtle energy centres in the body. Although you cannot see them, they connect your physical body with the subtle energetic bodies surrounding it, known as the aura or biomagnetic sheath. Each chakra links to a different area of life and to various issues and emotions (see table, pages 84–85).

The two chakras found below the waist – the base and sacral chakras – are positioned over the sexual organs. They connect with sexual and creative energy and are therefore known as the 'sexual' chakras. The solar plexus, heart and higher heart chakras are the emotional chakras, connecting with feelings and emotions. The throat and third eye are the mental chakras that allow expression of thoughts and feelings.

UNBLOCKING CHAKRAS

Chakras 'hold' feelings such as inadequacy, fear or anger and thoughts of resentment or guilt. This creates blockages in the flow of subtle energies, which in turn affects how you *feel* and how you respond to love.

Placing an appropriate crystal over a 'blocked' chakra can transform self-sabotaging behaviour, ingrained attitudes or thoughts and distressing feelings. Leave it in place for 10–15 minutes twice daily until the feeling dissipates. This may be almost instantaneous but usually takes about a week.

Many of the entries in this book indicate a chakra in connection with a crystal.

THE CHAKRAS

Crown At the top of the head, spiritual connection point

Soma At the hairline above the third eye, centre of spiritual identity and consciousness activation

Throat Over the physical throat, centre of truth

Heart Over the physical heart, love centre

Solar plexus Emotional centre

Sacral Just below the navel

Higher crown Above the crown, linkage point for spirit

Third eye Midway between eyebrows and hairline, centre of insight

Past life Just behind the ears, stores past-life information

Higher heart Over the thymus, centre of immunity

Spleen Under left armpit, potential site of energy leakage

Base At the perineum, sexual and creative centre

Earth Between the feet, linkage point to the earth

CHAKRA ASSOCIATIONS

Chakra	Colour	Position	Issue
Earth and higher earth	Brown	Below feet	Material connection
Base	Red	Base of spine	Survival instincts
Sacral	Orange	Below navel	Creativity and procreation
Solar plexus	Yellow	Above navel	Emotional connection and assimilation
Spleen	Light green	Under left arm	Energy leaching
Heart	Green	Over heart	Love
Higher heart	Pink	Over thymus	Unconditional love
Throat	Blue	Throat	Communication
Brow (third eye)	Dark blue	Forehead	Intuition and mental connection
Soma	Lavender	Centre of hairline	Spiritual connection
Past Life	Light turquoise-green	Behind ears	Anything carried over from past lives
Crown	Violet	Top of head	Spiritual connection
Higher Crown	White	Above head	Spiritual enlightenment

Positive Qualities	Negative Qualities
Grounded, practical, operates well in everyday reality	Ungrounded, no sense of power, cannot operate in everyday reality, picks up negativity
Base security, sense of one's own power, active, independant, spontaneous leadership	Impatience, fear of annihilation, death wish, over-sexed or impotent, vengeful, violence, anger, hyperactive, impulsive, manipulative
Fertility, courage, assertive, confident, joy, sexuality, sensual pleasure, acceptance of sexual identity	Low self-esteem, infertility, cruelty, inferiority, sluggishness, pompous, emotional hooks or thought forms
Good energy utilization, empathetic, organization, logic, active intelligence	Poor energy utilization, lazy, overly emotional or cold, cynical, emotional baggage, energy leaching, takes on other people's feelings and problems
Self-contained, powerful	Exhausted and manipulated
Loving, generous, compassionate, nurturing, flexible, self-confident, accepting	Disconnected from feelings, unable to show love, jealous, possessive, insecure, miserly or resistant to change
Compassionate, empathic, nurturing, forgiving, spiritually connected	Spiritually disconnected, grieving, inability to express feelings, needy
Able to speak own truth, receptive, idealistic, loyal	Unable to verbalize thoughts or feelings, stuck, dogmatic, disloyal
Intuitive, perceptive, visionary, in-the-moment	Spaced-out, fearful, attached to past, superstitious, bombarded with other people's thoughts
Spiritually aware and fully conscious	Cut off from spiritual nourishment and connectedness
Wisdom, life skills, instinctive knowing	Emotional baggage, insecurity, unfinished business
Mystical, creative, humanitarian, giving service	Overly-imaginative, illusory, arrogant, uses power to control others
Spiritual, attuned to higher things, enlightened, true humility	Spaced-out and open to invasion, illusions and delusions

FORGIVENESS

Forgiveness is essential if you are to be free to love fully. Being able to forgive and to accept forgiveness is a sign of emotional maturity and is part of a healthy relationship. You may need to forgive people from your past, or those in your present, and you may need to accept forgiveness from others.

Gentle pink Mangano Calcite is an excellent stone to carry with you for giving or receiving ongoing forgiveness. Use Rose Quartz, a stone of unconditional love and acceptance, in the 'Forgiveness ritual' below, as it brings about deep forgiveness and instils peace into your heart. Green Aventurine is a stone of compassion and empathy that also helps you to forgive others.

Rose Quartz

Forgiveness affirmation: 'My heart is filled with love and forgiveness. I forgive anyone who I feel has wronged me in the past or in the present, and I accept forgiveness from anyone I have wronged. I profoundly and deeply love, accept and forgive myself.'

Additional crystals: Rhodochrosite, Rhodonite, Chrysoberyl, Chrysoprase, Apache Tear (Translucent Obsidian), Infinite Stone, Rutilated Quartz, Larimar.

RITUAL: FORGIVENESS

Doing this ritual every time you feel angry or challenged is a great way to keep emotionally healthy and fully loving. The gentle energies of Rose Quartz help you to forgive both yourself and other people.

Most potent time: full moon (or whenever forgiveness is needed).

You will need:
1 Rose Quartz crystal
photograph of the person concerned (optional)

1. Hold a Rose Quartz over your higher heart chakra. Picture the person you feel you need to forgive or from whom you seek forgiveness, or use a photograph if you have one.

2. Be aware of the unconditionally loving energy of the Rose Quartz radiating out into your higher heart chakra and from there into your heart. Feel your heart filling with love and forgiveness. Be aware that this energy is also pouring into the other person's heart, which is opening and expanding to meet yours. Say out loud:

'I forgive you and I accept your forgiveness. I offer you unconditional love and acceptance. Go in peace.'

3. When you feel ready, put down the crystal but keep it visible to remind you of the forgiveness you have given and received.

CAN'T BELIEVE IT'S LOVE?

If you have difficulty believing someone when they say they love you and especially if, deep down inside, you secretly feel unlovable, crystals can transform how you feel about yourself. Stones gently transmute the past and enable you to move forward into a new way of loving.

LOVE YOURSELF

Accepting love from other people has to start with loving yourself. This is not a selfish love nor is it self-centred, it is self-enhancing. After all, if you don't love yourself, how can you believe that anyone else loves you? You will expect them to leave you and will unconsciously behave in ways that push them away. When they say: 'I can't stand this anymore' and storm off, you say to yourself: 'There, I knew they'd leave.' The tension that you were feeling dissipates and, even though you may feel devastated, part of you sighs with relief. If you are to enjoy a deep loving relationship, this pattern obviously needs to be broken.

Tender Pink Agate slowly but surely transforms your ability to accept love. This supportive stone helps you to accept yourself and the love that is your right. It is slow working and you need to wear it continuously or rub 10 drops of the gem essence (see page 16) over your heart three times a day for at least a month. Keeping the Pink Agate under your pillow is also beneficial.

Pink Agate

Repeating affirmations out loud to yourself is an excellent way of bringing new energy into your life and transforming how you feel about yourself. They have to be phrased in the present to work. Try repeating the 'Lovableness affirmation' out loud twice a day while looking into your eyes in a mirror and holding a Rose Quartz to your heart. Although it may feel strange – and untrue – at first, you will soon come to believe what you are saying. Believing it acts like a magnet for love.

Lovableness affirmation: 'I am lovable, I deserve love and I love myself deeply and unconditionally right now.'

Additional crystals: Rhodochrosite, Muscovite, Spirit Quartz, Blue Lace Agate, Larimar.

FOCUSING ON THE NOW

Living in the past and sighing for 'what could have been' is a dangerous practice if you desire love. It stops you seeing what could be in the present, as does carrying emotional baggage from the past. Letting go and focusing on the now is an extremely potent way to improve the amount of love in your life.

CLEARING EMOTIONAL BAGGAGE

Infinite Stone clears emotional baggage from previous relationships and resolves issues with people from your past, leaving you free to focus on the *now*. Wear one for a few weeks and you'll be surprised by how much more positive you feel and how much more alive to the present you feel.

Additional crystals: Halite, Pink Petalite, Pink Sapphire, Yellow Smithsonite.

Chakra: base, sacral, solar plexus.

Positive feelings: light and carefree.

Yellow Smithsonite

RITUAL: WASHING AWAY THE PAST

As you do this ritual, consciously focus on what you want to let go, giving it all to the cleansing flow.

Most potent time: full moon (but you can shower away the past whenever you become aware of holding on to it).

You will need:

1 Halite cluster

1. Stand under a shower to which you have attached a Halite cluster. As the water washes over the stone, it will dissolve and shower you with gentle cleansing energies.
   As it does so, say out loud:
   'I let go of the past and embrace the present. I choose to live in the unlimited possibilities of the eternal now.'

2. As you step out of the shower, be aware that you are stepping into the present, a space where all things can unfold and new love enters your life.

Halite

TRANSFORMING UNHARMONIOUS RELATIONSHIPS

Some relationships just never seem to go smoothly, they are a bumpy ride, and yet the two people love each other immensely and wouldn't want to part. But somehow they argue and fight their way through love, which can be utterly exhausting. Fortunately, if you find yourself in this situation, crystals can transform the situation and bring out the underlying love.

Rose Quartz has been used for thousands of years to harmonize and heal dysfunctional relationships. If you've found it difficult to maintain love, Sugilite brings about forgiveness and increases love, while, worn regularly, Chiastolite transforms conflict into loving harmony. These stones can be laid on a photograph of anyone with whom you have a relationship that doesn't work, to transform it into harmony.

Chiastolite

RITUAL: HEALING A RELATIONSHIP THAT DOESN'T WORK SMOOTHLY

This ritual is extremely effective if worked as a couple but you can also work it on your own, thinking of the other person with unconditional love as you do so.

Most potent time: new moon.

You will need:

pieces of Rose Quartz, Sugilite or Chiastolite photograph of yourself and the other person concerned additional gem essences (optional)

1. Place the photograph (use separate photographs if you do not have one of you together) in a quiet place where it will not be disturbed.

2. Lay pieces of the crystal you have chosen around the photograph(s), having already programmed the crystals (see page 15) to heal the relationship. Place one on the heart of each person. Leave in place until full moon.

3. Drop additional gem essences on to the crystals to introduce the vibrations of different stones if appropriate.

CRYSTALS TO ENHANCE POSITIVE ATTITUDE

Carrying a crystal with you or placing it over your heart chakra or solar plexus chakra enhances a positive attitude, as does rubbing the gem essence over these chakras. Clear Quartz is a master healer, which enhances all constructive emotions and attitudes and energizes you towards being positive. If it has rainbows inside, it brings great joy into your life and can be programmed to ensure a happy outcome.

Ametrine

SELF-ACCEPTANCE

Ametrine is an excellent stone for encouraging acceptance of yourself and of others. The stimulating yellow of Citrine combines with the loving energies of Amethyst to encourage you to open your heart to acceptance.

Additional crystals: Rose Quartz, Smoky Quartz, Hemimorphite, Agate, Carnelian, Muscovite.

Lapis Lazuli

EMOTIONAL HONESTY

Lapis Lazuli has the power to enhance your ability to be honest about your emotions while retaining sensitivity to how those feelings are being received so that you speak in a way that is heard.

Additional crystals: Jasper, Hemimorphite, Melanite Garnet, Topaz.

EMPATHY

Moonstone enhances sensitivity and empathy. Wearing Moonstone helps you feel how other people feel but if you are sensitive, especially at full moon, it may be better to choose a less sensitizing but equally empathetic stone.

Additional crystals: Rose Quartz, Malachite, Aventurine, Moldavite, Topaz, Brown Tourmaline.

Moonstone

SELF-EMPOWERMENT

If you need to feel empowered, keep Obsidian in your pocket.
Additional crystals: Sunstone, Smoky Amethyst, Tanzanite.

Obsidian

PATIENCE

If you suffer from chronic impatience, Emerald calms you down and instils serenity.

Additional crystals: Danburite, Green Tourmaline, Watermelon Tourmaline, Spirit Quartz.

Emerald

POTENTIAL

If you desire to enhance your potential, place a beautiful Dioptase crystal on your desk or find one that has been set as jewellery as this crystal is too fragile to carry in your pocket.

Additional crystals: Rhodonite, Hemimorphite, Herkimer Diamond, Moldavite, Opal, Aqua Aura.

Dioptase

SELF-RESPONSIBILITY

If you need to take more responsibility for yourself and your feelings, Malachite assists you.

Additional crystals: Citrine, Ocean Jasper, Hemimorphite, Aquamarine, Opal, Peridot, Snow Quartz, Royal Sapphire.

Malachite

CREATING LOVING AND POSITIVE SURROUNDINGS

crystals maintain harmonious
vibes and vibrant energies
in your surroundings

BRINGING LOVE INTO YOUR ENVIRONMENT

The delicate petals of a lilac Amethyst Flower-formation introduce light and love into your surroundings, while the womb-like interior of an Amethyst Geode encourages compatibility and harmony.

Amethyst is particularly effective if you need to bring a lighter vibration to your working environment – and if you desire to attract someone with whom you work. This stone has a dual action, also neutralizing geopathic stress (created by underground water and power lines, see page 105) or electromagnetic stress from computers, cell phones and televisions. Programme one to attract more love into your neighbourhood.

Amethyst Geode

Amethyst Flower

LOVE IN THE HOME

Crystals focus on love in your home and setting up an energy grid of crystals strengthens love and positive relationships. Triangulation layouts heighten the energy of stones, creating a grid that cleanses the energy and recharges the house with positive, unconditional loving vibrations.

Triangulation is particularly effective undertaken with Smoky Quartz laid at full moon to cleanse negativity and then repeated at new moon with Rose Quartz, which is left in place afterwards to bring in new loving energy (see page 100). You can also choose other stones to bring specific energies into your home or to protect against negative environmental energies or crime – for the latter use a grid of Sardonyx.

For an abundance of love and a wealth of good vibes place a large Citrine Geode in the abundance corner of your house (see the 'Love grid' right).

LOVE GRID

This is a permanent arrangement of crystals that creates an energy forcefield that draws in and maintains loving energies in your home. Lay the 'Love grid' over a plan of your home to help you position stones appropriately.

Abundance		Relationship corner
Ancestors and family life		Children
Helpful friends		

LAYOUT: ROSE QUARTZ TRIANGULATION LAYOUT

This layout of crystals will bring in new loving energy. Remember to cleanse the crystals regularly, always setting up the grid again afterwards. Do this once a week initially. Later, when your home feels good, once a month is enough.

Most potent time: new moon.

You will need:

3 large pieces of Rose Quartz

crystal wand (optional)

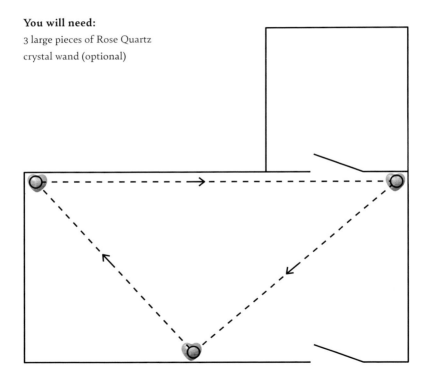

1. Place one large Rose Quartz in a central position, as close as possible to the front wall of the house.

2. Place a large Rose Quartz in each of the rear corners of the house, as close to the back wall as possible. Try to position the stones evenly – if your house has an L- or T-shaped extension, ignore the extension.

3. Now picture lines of force joining the stones in a triangle and passing through walls if necessary. If you have a crystal wand use this to connect the stones – touch a stone with the wand then carry the wand to the next stone in a straight line. If a wall prevents you from doing this, visualize the line of force you are creating going through the wall and start again on the other side of the wall.

4. Programme the crystals (see page 15) to emanate more and more love into the house.

LAYOUT: CREATING A SAFE AND LOVING SPACE

Gridding your house with Rose Quartz, Selenite or Smoky Quartz creates a very safe and loving space. Use either tumbled stones, chunks of the raw stone or shaped pieces, such as pyramids or balls. This layout can be adapted to a single room or to larger homes. It is not necessary to grid an upper storey as the energy grid created by the stones is multi-dimensional.

It's important to lay the stones in the order shown as this weaves the web, or forcefield, of loving energy you are creating as you walk. If you cannot walk directly to the next point, imagine the stone passing through a wall to create a straight line (and if possible place stones either side of the wall). Remember to connect point 5 to point 1.

Most potent time: new moon.

You will need:
5 Selenite, Rose or Smoky Quartz crystals
crystal wand (optional)

1. Visualize the layout opposite over a plan of a single room or your home, to help you position stones appropriately. Lay the first stone at point 1 on the diagram opposite.

2. Lay the second stone at point 2 on the diagram.

3. Lay the third stone at point 3 on the diagram.

4. Lay the fourth stone at point 4 on the diagram.

5. Lay the fifth stone at point 5 on the diagram.

6. Walk back to point 1 on the diagram.

7. If you have a crystal wand, walk the pentagram again, this time using the wand to connect up the stones (see the 'Rose Quartz triangulation layout', page 100).

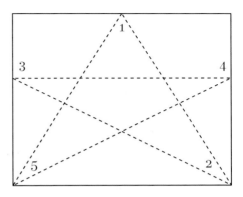

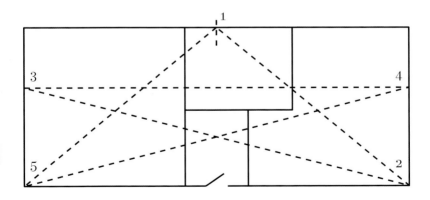

SENDING LOVE INTO THE WORLD

The more love that goes out to the world, the more loving your own world becomes – and the safer it feels to love, and everyone benefits. As more and more love is generated, love comes back to you in a self-replenishing cycle facilitated by the love crystals.

WORLD LOVE CRYSTALS

Rose Quartz is probably the best universal love stone there is. Programme one to send out love to the whole world, neutralizing terror and hostility wherever it finds it and replacing it with unconditional love and forgiveness. Picture this love radiating out from the stone until it surrounds the whole world and returns to you. Touch the stone each day and send more love out as you do.

A Selenite pillar, or a large Spirit Quartz cluster (see left), that has lots of tiny points wrapped around several big points to radiate love in all directions works equally well.

Additional crystals: Rhodochrosite, Danburite, Larimar, Elestial Quartz, Amethyst.

ENVIRONMENTAL POLLUTANTS

Modern life generates energetic pollution that subtly affects your sense of ease and well-being, and which can interfere with your sleep and your readiness to love. Crystals are extremely effective for neutralizing this energetic pollution and can be used in various ways.

One of the most effective methods is to place an appropriate crystal between you and the source of pollution, be it electricity pylons, a power station or a negative ley line. Negative ley lines are known as 'black energy lines' and are often created when underground water runs under ancient sites or where power lines run alongside homes. This can act like an energy drain and cause a subtle disease that disturbs your ability to feel comfortable in your own skin. Experienced dowsers can 'move' these lines if they fall close to homes, using the power of their mind, or 'pegs' such as pieces of copper or crystals, or other tools. However, crystals will reverse them into positive lines that create healing for the environment and for you.

CRYSTALS FOR REVERSING A NEGATIVE ENVIRONMENT

To reverse negative energies place Selenite or Black Tourmaline in a grid around your home. Selenite sends gentle white light and unconditional love out into the environment, creating harmony. Black Tourmaline blocks pollution and geopathic stress, and neutralizes ill wishing.

You can dowse (see page 12) to determine the placement of the crystals in your home or simply put one in each corner of a room. Grids are also extremely useful if you become the focus of someone wishing you ill as it blocks out bad vibes. Remember to cleanse and recharge stones used for combating environmental pollution regularly. You could also use any of the following crystals.

Amber

Amber

Amber creates a shield around you that feels rather like being encased in the sweetness of honey. It is strongly supportive and pours love into your environment.

Smoky Quartz

Smoky Quartz

An excellent neutralizer of negative environmental energies, Smoky Quartz draws off pollution, cleanses and re-energizes the whole space.

Green Aventurine

Green Aventurine

One of the most effective stones for neutralizing electromagnetic pollution, Green Aventurine also blocks geopathic stress and creates more love in your environment.

Larimar

An earth healing stone, Larimar helps women restore their connection with nature. Placed on the earth, it will counteract earth energy imbalances and geopathic stress.

Larimar

Opal

Opal sends healing to the earth's energy field, repairing depletions and re-energizing and stabilizing the energy grid that surrounds the earth.

Opal

Amethyst

Amethyst is an extremely powerful and protective stone, transmuting negativity into love. A natural tranquillizer, it blocks and reverses negative environment energies.

Amethyst

Turquoise

A purification stone that dispels negative energy and clears electromagnetic smog (created by computers, cell phones and other electronic equipment), Turquoise provides protection against environmental pollutants. Keep one on your computer.

Turquoise

Blue Sapphire

Traditionally associated with love and purity, Blue Sapphire is highly effective for earth healing and imparting tranquillity.

Blue Sapphire

Malachite

Particularly useful for blocking subtle nuclear radiation, Malachite should be placed between you and its source.

Malachite

LOVE
CRYSTALS
DIRECTORY

finding the right love crystal for your
needs will reap emotional rewards

DIRECTORY

Many of the major love crystals are multi-purpose. To find the right stone, look through the list of properties and select one that fulfils as many needs as possible. You can combine stones – Rose and Smoky Quartz work extremely well together, for instance. In some cases, such as Jasper and Agate, the generic stone is described here, so be guided by 'Additional crystals…' in the main body of the book as to specifics.

CLEAR CRYSTALS

Diamond

Diamond bonds relationships, brings love and clarity into a partnership and enhances the love of a husband for his wife. A sign of commitment and fidelity, Diamond clears emotional and mental pain, reduces fear and brings about new beginnings.

Brandenberg

Brandenberg is the most powerful reprogramming crystal available and is perfect for reframing vows and promises. Emanating infinite compassion, it facilitates deep soul healing and offers forgiveness and a tool for looking within yourself.

Selenite

Selenite is unconditional love solidified. Intuitive and loving communication is enhanced by two people each holding a piece. This stone assists in accessing your soul plan, pinpointing lessons and issues still being worked upon, and showing how they can best be resolved. A powerful disperser of negativity and stabilizer of erratic emotions, Selenite creates a protective grid around a house that prevents outside influences entering in. A large piece of Selenite placed in the home ensures a peaceful atmosphere. *Fragile, dissolves in water.*

Petalite is helpful during bond cutting and for neutralizing manipulation. Worn on a long chain over your heart, Petalite activates the energy centres of the body. It also enhances the environment by sending out loving energy and restoring harmony.

Petalite

Moonstone provides deep emotional healing. Placed on the solar plexus, it draws out old emotional patterning and makes conscious what has been unconscious. Fostering empathy, Moonstone calms over-reactions to situations and emotional triggers.

Moonstone

Spirit Quartz is full of unconditional love. Small points radiate love in all directions and a large point focuses it into your heart.

Opal has long been associated with love and passion, desire and eroticism. It intensifies emotional states, encourages positive emotions, releases inhibitions and acts as an emotional stabilizer but other stones may be needed to integrate. It shows what your emotional state has been in the past, especially in other lives, and teaches how to take responsibility for how you feel. Wearing Opal brings loyalty, faithfulness and spontaneity, but may amplify fickleness. Enhancing self-worth, it helps you to understand your full potential. Opals send healing to the earth's energy field, repairing depletions and re-energizing and stabilizing the energy grid that surrounds earth (similar to acupuncture energy meridians of our physical bodies). *Friable, damaged by water.*

Spirit Quartz

Opal

Rutilated Quartz Filtering negative energy, Rutilated Quartz supports your energy field during emotional release and confrontation with darker aspects of the psyche. It draws off disease from the past and promotes insights into events affecting the present, promoting forgiveness. This stone reaches the root of problems and facilitates transitions and a change of direction. Soothing dark moods, it acts as an antidepressant, relieving fears and anxiety, releasing constrictions and countering self-hatred.

Rutilated Quartz

PINK CRYSTALS

Rose Quartz

Rose Quartz Beautiful Rose Quartz is one of the most romantic of crystals and is prized for its unconditional love, heart healing and forgiveness. Nothing is more effective at attracting and maintaining love than Rose Quartz. It opens your heart centre, restoring love and trust. This stone teaches you how to love yourself and to receive love from someone else.

Danburite

Danburite Working on heart energy, Danburite smoothes the path ahead. It instils serenity and is an excellent stone for facilitating deep change and for leaving the past behind. It clears away any emotional or toxic debris from the past – whenever that might have been – and changes recalcitrant attitudes, instilling patience and peace of mind.

Rhodochrosite

Rhodochrosite Representing selfless love and compassion, Rhodochrosite imparts a dynamic and positive attitude towards life. It encourages spontaneous expression of feelings, including passionate and erotic urges. Lifting a depressed mood and bringing lightness into life, it is excellent for relationships, especially for people who feel unloved. This is the stone *par excellence* for healing sexual abuse. Rhodochrosite attracts a soulmate for your higher good. It teaches the heart to assimilate painful feelings without shutting down and removes denial. Gently bringing painful and repressed feelings to the surface, it allows them to be acknowledged and dissipated through emotional release. Rhodochrosite identifies ongoing patterns and shows the purpose behind experiences. This stone insists you face the truth, about yourself and other people, without excuses or evasion but with loving awareness. It improves self-worth and dissipates emotional stress.

Pink Tourmaline

Pink Tourmaline This beautiful stone stimulates your libido and encourages you to share physical pleasure with your lover. It is particularly effective made into a gem essence and rubbed on your wrists before bed. It is also an excellent heart healer.

Cobalto-Calcite (Cobaltite) Symbolizing unconditional love and forgiveness, Cobalto-Calcite is excellent for emotional healing. It soothes intense feelings, assisting you to love yourself and others, and to feel good about your life.

Cobalto-Calcite

Mangano Calcite A heart crystal and stone of forgiveness, gentle Mangano Calcite releases fear and grief that keep the heart trapped in the past, bringing in unconditional love. It assists in recovering self-worth and self-acceptance. Mangano Calcite's loving energy gently dissolves resistance. It is helpful for anyone who has suffered trauma, abuse or assault.

Mangano Calcite

Pink Sapphire This stone acts as a magnet to draw into your life all that you need in order to grow emotionally. A fast-acting stone, it teaches how to master emotions, clearing emotional blockages and abuse, and integrating the transmuted energies.

Pink Sapphire

Kunzite Pink Kunzite is an excellent healer for depression following break-up of a relationship. If your heart is full of emotional debris, tranquil Pink Kunzite dissolves it and brings in unconditional love to heal your heart.

Kunzite

Pink Crackle Quartz Formed from quartz that has been superheated and then dipped in pink dye to make it crack and turn pink, Pink Crackle Quartz promotes fun and joy in life. An excellent companion for life-enhancing pursuits that help you to recharge, it can also heal an abused or emotionally damaged child or inner child.

Pink Crackle Quartz

Muscovite

Muscovite opens your heart to intimate sharing. Facilitating accepting people's foibles, it stimulates unconditional love. It offers support during the exploration of painful feelings and facilitates clear expression. This stone disperses insecurity and self-doubt, and eliminates anger. It helps you look forward joyfully to the future and back to the past to appreciate all the lessons that have been learned. Muscovite relieves tectonic plate tensions within the earth. *Friable.*

Halite

Halite When placed in the environment, Pink Halite promotes a sense of being loved. A stone of purification, it protects against negative energies and dissolves old behavioural patterns and ingrained feelings such as anger. It can be placed in the bath or shower for this purpose. Ameliorating feelings of abandonment or rejection, this stone helps you transcend your problems. *Dissolves in water.*

Morganite

Morganite (Pink Beryl) Morganite attracts and maintains love. It encourages loving thoughts and actions, creating space to enjoy life and living. Activating and cleansing the heart chakra, Morganite is a powerful stone for dissolving conscious or unconscious resistance to transformation, clearing victim mentality and opening the heart to receive unconditional love. Morganite also assists in recognizing unfulfilled emotional needs and unexpressed feelings.

Smithsonite

Smithsonite Ideal for anyone who has had a difficult childhood and who felt unloved or unwanted, Smithsonite heals the inner child and alleviates the effects of emotional abuse and misuse. It dissolves emotional hurt so that you feel better rather than having traumatic emotional release. Smithsonite assists difficult relationships. Excellent for a secure and balanced life, it imparts harmony. **Lavender-Pink Smithsonite** has a particularly loving vibration. It heals the heart and experiences of abandonment and abuse, rebuilding trust and security, and assisting in feeling loved and supported by the universe. *Fragile.*

RED CRYSTALS

Rhodonite is a useful first aid measure for heart healing or for traumatic emotions. An emotional balancer, it brings your heart back online and is helpful when you have been betrayed. Being red, Rhodonite also stimulates passion and fires up your energy.

Rhodonite

Red Jasper A powerful re-energizer for stimulating libido and for prolonging sexual pleasure, Red Jasper energizes and cleanses the sex organs and is particularly appropriate for men.

Red Jasper

Red Garnet Stimulating passion and increasing sexual potency, Red Garnet has long been a symbol of love and devotion. It is a useful revitalizer.

Red Garnet

Ruby Imparting vigour to life, Ruby energizes and balances but may overstimulate irritable people. It encourages passion for life, stimulating the heart chakra and balancing the heart. Ruby brings up anger for transmutation and encourages removal of anything negative from your path. A sociable stone that attracts sexual activity, it overcomes lethargy and imparts potency and vigour.

Ruby

ORANGE CRYSTALS

Orange Carnelian A recharging crystal, vibrant Orange Carnelian energizes the creative centres, overcomes impotence or frigidity, and restores vitality to the female reproductive organs.

Orange Carnelian

YELLOW CRYSTALS

Sunstone

Sunstone A joyful, light-inspiring stone, Sunstone instils *joie de vivre*. If life has lost its sweetness, Sunstone restores it and helps you to nurture yourself. This stone allows the real self to shine out. It removes 'hooks' from possessive lovers that drain your energy, and is beneficial for bond cutting. Keep Sunstone with you if you have difficulty in saying 'no'. Removing co-dependency, it facilitates self-empowerment, independence and vitality. Sunstone is an anti-depressant and lifts dark moods. It detaches you from feeling abandoned. Removing inhibitions and hang-ups, Sunstone increases self-worth and confidence. Encouraging optimism and enthusiasm, it switches you to a positive take on events. Placed on the solar plexus, Sunstone lifts out heavy or repressed emotions and transmutes them.

Citrine

Citrine A powerful cleanser, Citrine is extremely protective for the environment. Gloom and negativity have no place around Citrine, which promotes joy in life. It releases negative traits, overcomes fear of responsibility and stops anger. This stone helps you move into the flow of feelings and become emotionally balanced. Citrine raises self-esteem and self-confidence, and removes destructive tendencies. It enhances individuality and encourages self-expression, making you less sensitive to criticism. This stone helps you develop a positive attitude and to look forward optimistically instead of hanging on to the past. Citrine encourages exploring every possible avenue until you find the best solution. Wearing a Citrine pendant overcomes difficulty in verbalizing thoughts and feelings.

Topaz

Topaz An empathetic stone that stimulates, recharges and remotivates, Topaz promotes truth, forgiveness and trust. Supporting affirmations, manifestation and visualization, Topaz helps you discover your own inner riches. Topaz makes you feel confident, and negativity does not survive around the joyful stone. It promotes openness and honesty, self-realization and self-control. It is also an excellent emotional support, stabilizing the emotions and making you receptive to love.

Yellow Jasper channels positive energy and cleanses the solar plexus chakra. Known as the 'Supreme Nurturer', Jasper sustains and supports during times of stress. It reminds humanity to aid each other, brings the courage to get to grips with problems assertively, and encourages honesty with yourself and with others.

Yellow Jasper

Beryl (see Morganite) Vibrant Beryl reawakens love in long-term partners whose relationship feels jaded. This stone helps you shed unnecessary baggage. Discouraging overanalysis and anxiety, it encourages a positive view.

Beryl

Yellow Smithsonite balances the solar plexus chakra and releases old hurts and outgrown emotional patterning.

Yellow Smithsonite

PURPLE CRYSTALS

Sugilite opens all the chakras to the flow of love. Teaching how to live from your truth and reminding the soul of its reasons for incarnating, it brings light and love into the darkest situations. Fostering forgiveness and eliminating hostility, Sugilite encourages loving communication. This stone imparts the ability to face up to unpleasant matters and alleviates sorrow, grief and fears, promoting self-forgiveness. It overcomes conflict without either party having to compromise.

Sugilite

Amethyst is an extremely powerful and protective stone, transmuting negativity into love. A natural tranquillizer, it blocks negative environment energies. Amethyst balances out highs and lows, aiding emotional centering. It dispels anger, rage, fear and anxiety. Alleviating sadness and grief, it supports coming to terms with loss.

Amethyst

Tanzanite is a useful past life healer, instilling trust and overcoming depression and anxiety. It creates a space for new patterns to be integrated. Tanzanite jewellery should be worn with care as it may overstimulate sensitive people.

Tanzanite

BLUE CRYSTALS

Sapphire

Sapphire releases unwanted thoughts, bringing serenity. This stone dissolves depression and assists self-expression. Wear Sapphire touching the body. **Blue Sapphire** is traditionally associated with love and purity. It is highly effective for earth and chakra healing. This tranquil stone transmutes negative energies and facilitates speaking your own truth. **Royal Sapphire** teaches responsibility for your thoughts and feelings.

Lapis Lazuli

Lapis Lazuli Dedicated to Venus, Roman goddess of love, for over five thousand years, Lapis Lazuli helps you take charge of life and bonds love and friendship. It reveals inner truth and encourages self-expression without holding back or compromising. If repressed anger is causing difficulties, Lapis Lazuli releases this. This stone brings honesty, compassion and uprightness to a relationship. It helps you confront truth, wherever you find it, and accept what it teaches. Lapis Lazuli harmonizes conflict and teaches the value of active listening. It clears martyrdom, cruelty and suffering. As a gem essence, it dissolves emotional bondage.

Crystalline Kyanite

Crystalline Kyanite To the sensitive eye, bright and sparky Crystalline Kyanite gives off sparks of energy and some people can feel a tingle. It smoothes the way for lasting relationships, for which two stones are needed – one for each person. The stones can be programmed to enhance intuitive communication between two people and to bring harmony and unconditional love to a partnership.

Hemimorphite encourages accepting responsibility for your own happiness, and teaches that you create your own reality through thoughts and attitudes. Teaching how to develop your own inner strength and manifest your highest potential, Hemimorphite gently soothes emotional angst. If you invariably pitch your expectations and goals too high to achieve, Hemimorphite helps you to set, and attain, realistic goals. This stone helps you look back on, and reframe, irritating traits, and facilitates being totally open and honest in your emotional communication. *Fragile, so use tumbled stone.*

Hemimorphite

Blue Lace Agate A nurturing and supportive stone, Blue Lace Agate neutralizes feelings of anger. It counteracts the suppression of feelings that stem from fear of being judged and rejected, and overcomes self-sabotage. Blue Lace Agate gently encourages a new mode of expression.

Blue Lace Agate

Larimar Radiating love and peace, Larimar is an excellent stone for those seeking a soulmate. Facilitating healing past life relationships or heart trauma, it reconnects you to natural playfulness and joyful child energy. This stone removes self-imposed blockages and constraints and dissolves self-sabotaging behaviour, especially martyrdom, and assists in taking control of life. It alleviates guilt and removes fear, and is an antidote to emotional extremes. An earth healing stone, Larimar connects to the original earth mother goddess, helping women reattune to their innate femininity. Placed on the earth – out in a park or the country if you don't have a garden, or in a pot of earth on your windowsill – it counteracts earth energy imbalances and geopathic stress.

Larimar

BLUE-GREEN CRYSTALS

Turquoise

Turquoise stimulates romantic love, enhancing communication and empathy. It is believed to change colour to warn of infidelity. A purification stone that dispels negative energy and clears electromagnetic smog, it provides protection against environmental pollutants. Turquoise dissolves a martyred attitude or self-sabotage and is excellent for exhaustion, depression or panic attacks.

Aquamarine

Aquamarine Invoking tolerance of others, Aquamarine overcomes judgementalism, supporting anyone overwhelmed by responsibility and encourages taking responsibility for yourself. Creating a personality that is upright, persistent and dynamic, it breaks old, self-defeating pre-programmed behaviour. Bringing unfinished business to a conclusion, Aquamarine facilitates closure on all levels. It clears blocked communication and assists self-expression. This stone helps in understanding how you feel. It soothes fears, and increases sensitivity.

Dioptase

Dioptase A powerful healer for the heart, Dioptase supports a positive attitude, instils an ability to tune into your own resources, and releases the need to control others. Its green ray reaches deep within the heart, absorbing festering wounds and forgotten hurts. It dissolves grief, betrayal and sorrow, and heals heartache and the pain of abandonment. Dioptase teaches that ultimately pain and difficulty in relationship mirrors inner separation from yourself. Repairing that link and drawing in love at all levels, it heals an emotional black hole that is desperate for love. This stone clears away perceptions as to how love ought to be and brings in a new vibration of love. *Fragile.*

Blue-Green
Smithsonite

Blue-Green Smithsonite This stone heals emotional and other wounds by bringing in universal love. Gently releasing anger, fear and pain, it assists in attaining your heart's desire.

GREEN CRYSTALS

Emerald The 'stone of successful love', Emerald encourages domestic bliss and loyalty. It enhances unity, unconditional love and partnership, keeping a relationship in balance. Said to signal unfaithfulness if it changes colour, Emerald opens the heart chakra and calms emotions. It enhances the ability to enjoy life to the full.

Emerald

Green Tourmaline opens the heart chakra, promoting compassion, tenderness, patience and a sense of belonging. This nurturing stone brings balance and *joie de vivre*. Transforming negative to positive and dispelling fears, Green Tourmaline promotes openness and patience and assists visualization.

Green Tourmaline

Green Aventurine A comforter, heart healer and general harmonizer, Aventurine gently dissolves distressing feelings and thoughts. This stone strengthens mature love and is excellent for transmuting negative earth energies.

Green Aventurine

Peridot A powerful cleanser, Peridot activates the heart and solar plexus chakras and releases 'old baggage'. Clearing burdens, guilt or obsessions and releasing negative patterns, Peridot teaches that holding on to people or the past is counter-productive. Peridot alleviates jealousy, resentment and anger. It enhances confidence and assists in looking back to the past to find the gift in your experiences. Showing how to forgive yourself, it brings to your attention all the things you have neglected. With the assistance of Peridot, you admit mistakes and move on. It helps take responsibility for your own life and avoid blaming others. Peridot greatly improves difficult relationships.

Peridot

Malachite

Malachite opens the heart to unconditional love. It rapidly absorbs negative energies and pollutants. A stone of transformation, Malachite draws out deep feelings, trauma and psychosomatic causes, breaks unwanted bonds and outworn patterns, and teaches responsibility for your actions, thoughts and feelings. This stone develops empathy, showing how it would feel to be in other people's place. Malachite is helpful for psycho-sexual problems, especially when caused by traumatic previous life sexual experiences. *Toxic, use tumbled stone.*

Green Sapphire

Green Sapphire stimulates the heart chakra, bringing loyalty, fidelity and integrity to a relationship. This stone enhances compassion and understanding the frailty and unique qualities of others. It honours trust and other people's belief systems.

Variscite

Variscite restores libido, increases sexual energy and brings unconditional love into any situation. This stone facilitates moving out of deep despair into hope and trust. It does away with pretence, enabling you to show yourself to the world exactly as you are.

Infinite Stone

Infinite Stone helps you access and integrate past, present and future and is excellent for past life exploration, promoting compassion and forgiveness for yourself and what you went through. This stone heals imbalances from past lives and clears emotional baggage from previous relationships. Placed on the throat, it facilitates speaking of the past and resolves issues carried over into the present. Use Infinite Stone if you need to confront anyone from your past as it brings a gentle touch to the meeting.

DARK-COLOURED CRYSTALS

Smoky Quartz A strong detoxifier and negative energy absorber, Smoky Quartz purifies and re-energizes you and your environment. If you have hang-ups about sexual matters, Smoky Quartz helps you accept that sex is a normal, natural and highly enjoyable part of life. It enhances virility and cleanses the sexual centres so that passion flows freely.

Smoky Quartz

Agate Strong but slow working, Agate heals bitterness of the heart and draws out distressing feelings. It is particularly useful when heartbreak is deeply entrenched and accompanied by resentment or betrayal. It dissolves anger and gives courage to start again. Agate comes in many forms and colours (see Pink Agate and Blue Lace Agate). **Banded Agate** sets you free from past connections and all Agates overcome self-sabotage.

Agate

Obsidian A fast-acting stone, Obsidian draws out and dissolves painful memories and distressing feelings. It tends to surface things fast and you may need other crystals to help heal the heart afterwards.

Obsidian

Rainbow Obsidian Beautiful banded Rainbow Obsidian acts gently to release past pain, cutting the cords of old love and removing hooks that others have left in your heart. It clears emotional bondage.

Rainbow Obsidian

Red-Black Obsidian This powerful stone increases virility and stamina, keeping you grounded in your body so that sex becomes a full-body experience. It raises the kundalini energy (sexual energy that rises up the spine from the base to the top of the head, and which is stimulated by tantric sex, some yoga and meditation practices) and promotes vitality and virility.

Red-Black Obsidian

Mahogany
Obsidian

Cymophane

Tiger's Eye

Sardonyx

Pietersite

Mahogany Obsidian Resonating with the earth, stabilizing Mahogany Obsidian grounds and protects, offers strength in times of need, vitalizes purpose, eliminates energy blockages, and stimulates growth on all levels.

Cymophane A form of Cat's Eye, Cymophane supports flexibility of mind and enhances unconditional love.

Tiger's Eye A protective stone, Tiger's Eye assists in accomplishing goals and brings clarity of intention and integrity. Placed on the sacral chakra, Tiger's Eye is excellent for people who are uncommitted. This stone facilitates recognizing your own needs and those of others. It differentiates between wishful thinking and what you really need. Tiger's Eye heals issues of self-worth and self-criticism and assists in recognizing your faults that need to be overcome. It alleviates depression and lifts moods.

Sardonyx is a stone of strength that promotes integrity and virtuous conduct. Bringing lasting happiness and stability to marriage and partnerships, Sardonyx attracts friends and good fortune. A protective stone that can be laid in a grid around the house and garden to prevent crime, it increases stamina, vigour and self-control. This stone alleviates depression and overcomes hesitancy.

Pietersite promotes walking your own truth, that is, following a pathway in accordance with your own beliefs and soul path. An extremely supportive and strengthening stone, it assists in speaking out and in processing ancient conflicts and suppressed feelings. This stone dispels the illusion of separateness and removes beliefs and conditioning imposed by other people. It releases you from vows such as celibacy and promises made in other lives that have carried over into the present life.

COMBINATION CRYSTALS

Ametrine A combination of Amethyst and Citrine, Ametrine is a dual stone that draws people together and enhances compatibility, enabling you to accept with love other people's flaws and fallibilities and to transmute your own distressing feelings. It is a powerful stone for energy purification and harmonization. Fast and effective in its action, Ametrine enhances compatibility and acceptance of others. It overcomes prejudice. An extremely energetic stone, it stimulates creativity and supports taking control of your own life. Emotionally, Ametrine releases blockages including distressing feelings and expectations, facilitating transformation, and brings insight into underlying causes of emotional distress.

Ametrine

Watermelon Tourmaline The 'super-activator' of the heart chakra, Watermelon Tourmaline fosters love, tenderness and friendship. This stone instils patience. Alleviating depression and fear, it promotes inner security and assists in understanding situations and clearly expressing intentions. Watermelon Tourmaline treats emotional dysfunction and releases old pain, and is beneficial for relationships and for finding the joy in situations.

Watermelon
Tourmaline

Shiva Lingam Symbolizing the god Shiva and union with his consort, Kali, a Shiva Lingam is used to raise and control kundalini energy. This stone has been revered for thousands of years as a symbol of sexuality and potent male energy. Excellent for sexual healing if suitably programmed, a Shiva Lingam severs subtle sexual connection after a relationship has ceased and removes hooks from vagina or uterus, re-energizing the base chakras and opening the way for a new relationship. A stone of insight, it facilitates looking within so that you release all that is outgrown. This stone dissolves emotional pain arising from early childhood, especially from sexual abuse, as it reinstates trust in male energy.

Shiva Lingam

INDEX

The Publisher would like to thank Earthworks and Mysteries for the kind loan of crystals for photography.

AUTHOR ACKNOWLEDGEMENTS

Judy Hall would like to honour the expertise and intuition of Jacqui Malone for triangulation and thank her for much else besides.

PICTURE ACKNOWLEDGEMENTS

Special photography: © Octopus Publishing Group Limited/Russell Sadur. All other photography: © Octopus Publishing Group Limited.

iStock: Helin Loik-Tomson 13, JulyProkopiv 2, 28, KrivoTIFF 58, Marilyn Nieves 17, Netrun78 15, 22, PamWalker68 87
Unsplash: Chelsea shapouri 16, Edz Norton 11, Laura Olsen 47, Susanna Marsiglia 20

RESOURCES

Good quality crystals can be obtained from www.exquisitecrystals.com (USA), www.crystalmaster.co.uk, from suppliers recommended by www.earthworksuk.com, or from Mysteries in London: www.mysteries.co.uk

OTHER BOOKS BY JUDY HALL

The Crystal Bible, Godsfield Press 2003
Crystal Healing, Godsfield Press 2005
Good Vibrations, Archive Publishing 2006
New Crystals and Healing Stones, Godsfield Press 2006
Manifesting with Crystals, Godsfield Press 2022
Crystals for Beginners; A Card Deck, Godsfield Press 2022
Judy Hall's Crystal Companion, Godsfield Press 2024